Running a Home-based Business

Business Enterprise Guides

Published in association with *The Sunday Times*

All titles are available from good bookshops. To obtain further information, please contact the publisher at the following address:

Kogan Page Ltd
120 Pentonville Road
London N1 9JN
Tel: 020 7278 0433
Fax: 020 7837 6348
www.kogan-page.co.uk

THE SUNDAY TIMES

BUSINESS ENTERPRISE GUIDE

Running a Home-based Business

2ND EDITION

DIANE BAKER

KOGAN
PAGE

First published in 1994
Reprinted with revisions 1996
Second edition 2002

Kogan Page Limited
120 Pentonville Road
London N1 9JN

British Library Cataloguing in Publication Data

A CIP record for this book is available from the British Library.

ISBN 0 7494 3665 4

Typeset by Jean Cussons Typesetting, Diss, Norfolk
Printed and bound in Great Britain by Thanet Press Ltd, Margate

need a **better** planned
workspace
at home?

sharps
HOME OFFICE

THE HOME OFFICE THAT HELPS RUN YOUR BUSINESS!

Working is easier and more comfortable with a Sharps Home Office.
Anyone who runs a business from home knows that trying to work in cramped, uncomfortable conditions can significantly reduce productivity and output. It's vital, therefore, to find a design solution that combines high levels of personal comfort with sufficient space and storage capacity to cope with your filing, documentation and P.C. equipment needs.

The Sharps Home Office – organised, attractive, and optimising available space
So if you're looking for a home office environment which is organised, attractive – and makes maximum use of available space – you can't make a better choice than Sharps, the UK's number one fitted furniture specialist. With a long-standing reputation for premium quality furniture, attractive designs, plus first class customer service, Sharps offers home workers the chance to create an efficient, effective & hard-working office area anywhere in the home.

Visit your nearest Sharps Home Office showroom
The best place to start is by visiting your nearest Sharps Home Office showroom (there's over 170 showrooms throughout the UK, so there's bound to be one near you), where you'll be able to see an extensive choice of styles and designs on display, together with a range of accessories which Sharps can also provide.

Sharps – working with you to plan your perfect home office
The next step is a free home visit from one of our consultants, who will discuss your needs with you and undertake a thorough survey of your potential home office area. Calling on the skills of Sharp's expert designers, your consultant will work with you to design a home office which meets all your needs, whether you're planning to work on your own, with colleagues or with other members of your family. Each Sharps Home Office is individually designed, combining aesthetics with practical considerations such as storage and shelf space, plenty of open working areas - even a meeting area – plus, of course, the all-important computer work station, which is at the heart of virtually all home offices nowadays.

Creating a brilliant home office anywhere in your home
With their unique and remarkable planning skills, it's amazing how Sharps can create a fully functioning home office in virtually any space, from alcoves and under-stair areas to entire rooms, under sloping eaves and in irregular-shaped corners – and always with an eye to attractive design, good looks, plus total practicality.

Wake up and work!

As well as being experts in home office design, Sharps are specialists in fitted bedroom design and installation, through their sister company Sharps Bedrooms. Utilising the skills of both companies, Sharps can now offer an exclusive design and build service in which a fitted bedroom can also incorporate a fully fitted office. So you can simply roll out of bed, take a few steps across the room – and you're in the office, ready to work!

A great choice of styles, finishes and storage solutions

As well as giving you total freedom to select the style and location of your home office environment, Sharps give you an extensive choice of good-looking finishes to choose from, such as oak, maple, pine and alder – plus an extensive selection of attractive handle styles. In addition, you can choose from standard or extra-deep desks, as well as extending equipment shelves and suspension file drawers. And as if that wasn't enough storage space, your Sharps Home Office can also incorporate floor-to-ceiling cupboards, hanging wall cupboards, open units and a variety of shelving systems.

Keeping your computer under control

Sharps home office designs also take into account computers, allowing for plenty of siting space for screens, as well as sliding trays for keyboards, plus integral cable management systems which ensure that cables are hidden so that desktops stay tidy and organised. Removable panels fitted in the knee-hole area can be easily removed, for access to neatly hidden plug and socket systems.

Expert installation – affordable prices

Delivery and installation is carried out free of charge by Sharps' experienced craftsmen, normally within three weeks of your order being placed. Fitting is usually completed in one day, with the minimum amount of disruption to the busy life of the household, and Sharps Home Offices are covered by a five-year guarantee. You'll also be pleased to know that Sharps Home Office prices are remarkably affordable, and with an extra £100 off all orders of £1000 or more – if you mention this feature – there's never been a better time to move up to a better way of working at home.

For your nearest showroom and a FREE colour brochure call

0800 32 32 32
or visit www.sharps.co.uk

 clearspace³

clear for work
space for living

Clearspace³ is a leading designer and supplier of furniture for the home office. Our products are:

- Functional
- Versatile
- Affordable
- Guaranteed for 5 years
- Compliant with all BS levels

Clearspace³ values your home and your office space. That is why our furniture integrates with either use seamlessly.

www.clearspace3.com

Monitored Security – Good for Business

Making the decision to run a business from home often comes after careful consideration. With so many things to think about, security may not be at the top of your list – until you have a break in. It is a sad fact, but most burglar alarms are only installed after a burglary.

If you have already made the wise investment of a burglar alarm, can you be certain that the Police will know if your home has been broken into? The only way you can be sure, is to have an intruder alarm that is monitored. What's more, a monitored alarm can not only look after your possessions, office equipment and files but your home and personal safety as well.

The Myth of ringing bells

A traditional burglar alarm tries to scare off intruders by the noise of a ringing bell or siren. But did you know that these traditional ringing alarms cannot ensure a response from the Police? If you were lucky, one of your neighbours might phone them to report the alarm, but the Police may only respond if someone can actually tell them there has been a burglary or an attempted burglary at your home.

Monitoring means a guaranteed responseA monitored alarm can help protect your home and family around the clock. If your alarm is activated, you can be assured of the right help – quickly.

You're connected 24 hours a day to a fully manned Alarm Receiving Centre via your phone line and if your system is activated, the Centre will know about it straight away. Within seconds they will call your home to verify the alarm (to help filter out false alarms) and where appropriate, will summon help immediately.

Good news for your neighbours

Monitored alarms don't always need a loud external siren, so there's no noise to annoy your neighbours. An internal siren is used as a deterrent to intruders to let them know that the alarm has been activated.

Twice as good

Monitored alarms can also help you guard against personal attack and fire, or even obtain emergency support from a designated friend or neighbour

Panic buttons can be added enabling you to summon help if you are attacked at home. Some systems let you send a secret signal if an intruder forced you to switch off your alarm against your will.

Many homes have battery-powered smoke detectors, but all too often the batteries are dead. Adding monitored smoke or fire detectors to a system can help protect your home from the threat of fire 24 hours a day, even if your alarm is not switched on.

Reducing False Alarms

In England, Wales and Northern Ireland, Police Policy states that new monitored alarm systems have to be 'confirmed'. This means an Alarm Receiving Centre can only report a break-in to the Police if they receive a signal from two separate detectors, which 'confirms' the break-in. This was introduced to cut down the number of false calls that the Police attend, so they can deploy their resources more effectively.

How do I get a monitored alarm?

Most companies will visit your home to conduct a free no-obligation survey, to find out your specific security needs and design a system to suit you. Choose a reputable company, which is independently regulated (look out for ones that are approved by NACOSS or SSAIB). This will ensure that your installation is of the highest quality and that your monitored alarm will qualify for Police response. Some companies have their own Alarm Receiving Centres whereas others use a third party, so be sure to check.

Having a monitored alarm will require you to have keyholders – people whom you have designated to hold keys to your home. When your alarm is activated (and if you cannot be contacted) one of your keyholders will be asked to provide access for the emergency services - they do not have to put themselves in harm's way. Keyholders should live nearby and know how to operate your alarm system!

How much?

For a monitored alarm system you will usually pay an up-front installation cost and an ongoing monthly charge for monitoring and maintenance. Prices will vary according to the amount of detection equipment that is installed.

Having an approved monitored alarm may enable you to qualify for a discount off your house insurance policy.

A monitored security system is capable of fending off more than just burglars and can summon help when you need it most. It is the wisest choice for looking after your home-based business and your loved ones. Who knows, it may even help you sleep a little easier.

ADDITIONAL INFO
Did you know?
In 1999, the chance of being burgled was 1 in 23
51% or burglaries happen when people are at home
1 in 8 adults worry about their homes being burgled
Homes with Security devices are effective in reducing the risk of burglary

Contents

Consumer legislation 139; Food safety 141; Disclosure of
information on business stationery 142

visionary stationery:

from a paperclip to a desk 100's of solutions

bureau

the home office store

bureau – the visionary stationery and furniture store

'Stuffed to the gills with everything under the stationery umbrella. In short the Conran Shop meets Ryman.' The Independent.

It is highly likely if you are running a home based business, and particularly if you are setting up or growing the company, that you will be pushed for time. bureau was designed specifically as a 'one-stop' shopping experience catering for every home office stationery and furniture requirement, saving professional home workers valuable shopping time that can be dedicated to making a success of their business. From paperclips through to furniture and filing solutions, for the first time everything can be found under one roof.

The benefits of working from home are obvious. No peak time rush and road-rage commuting, working to your own more productive schedule rather than having one dictated to you, and avoiding unhealthy air conditioning and lighting. You can even wear pyjamas if you want. There can, however, be drawbacks. It can be difficult to shut up shop and switch off, and there is a danger that your office just grows and grows. The bureau team believes that regardless of what form it takes, to combat this happening a home based office needs to be highly organised and practical, and that it should be housed in a clearly designated area that enables you to keep work separate from home life. The best news of all is that at bureau you don't need a massive budget or unlimited space to create an attractive and highly functional office.

bureau furniture

bureau has an extensive furniture catalogue with hundreds of desk combinations to fit just about any space. Whether you need a simple computer workstation or something much larger, bureau will be able to provide it. The best contemporary designs are sourced from all over Europe in various materials and finishes, and have matching filing cabinets and cupboards to create a total look. It is possible to order one desk or multiples if you have a larger home office, and most items are delivered and installed free of charge in mainland U.K. Forget struggling with heavy flat packs and complicated assembly instructions, visit bureau for an easier life.

bureau stores

Another bonus of having a home based office is that you can create a highly personal, welcoming and attractive workspace that appeals directly and individually to you. In fact it is an essential element in making sure that you get out of bed and make it into the office at all. Impose your personality in the home office and productivity and creativity will flourish. bureau positively encourages this by sourcing and stocking every stationery item you could possibly require in a massive range of colours, materials and textures. It's all about choice and you are positively challenged to find exactly the right pens, books, diary, folders, clock, calculator, lamp, bin and presentation files to suit you. There are often design-led gems to be found among even the most basic home office essentials.

The paperless office is a myth and as such practical filing and storage are essential for every office. If you are short on space bureau is the best place for mobile, wall mounted or under desk filing units. There is also a vast range of durable storage and archive boxes to keep papers and records from spreading and looking messy.

bureau business to business services

Complementing the bureau stores and extensive furniture catalogue there is a dedicated business to business team, providing customers with creative solutions to all of their promotional, presentation and packaging needs. The team can aid in the design of unique bespoke product and manufacture almost any item to exact specification. The b2b team are flexible and have worked on projects as diverse as providing 20,000 printed polypropylene training packs for a high street bank, through to 150 paper press packs for a home based PR consultancy. They also have the contacts and experience necessary to source suitable corporate gifts. Alternatively if there is a particular stock item from the store that is required in bulk the team will ensure it is made possible.

Stores can be visited in Covent Garden and Reading (please see advertisement for addresses, or a full furniture catalogue can be requested by talking to a member of the bureau team on 020 7836 3502.

1   *Choosing a home-based business*

What is a home-based business?

A home-based business can be almost anything you want it to be. One of its great advantages is the flexibility of working hours and the choice of businesses available.

In everyday terms, a home-based business means working for yourself, using your home as a workbase. It may be that you are working at home all day or are merely using your own telephone to take business calls, while your work is carried out at your customers' homes or premises.

Is there a home-based business suitable for me?

Almost certainly. There are so many different types of business to choose from that you should be able to find something appropriate to your skills and interests.

A home-based business will also be extremely flexible, enabling you to work the hours you want, when you want. You can, therefore, fit in running your business with a full- or part-time job, caring for children or other dependent relatives and pursuing your hobbies. Thus a home-based business can be a fulfilling complement to the other elements of your life.

You do, however, need to be determined, flexible, hard working and not want to be a millionaire, although this is a remote possibility! Working from home is not a soft option but it can be rewarding.

What are the advantages?

The main reasons people are attracted to running a business from home are that they will be working for themselves and working the hours they choose, so a home-based business can be run to fit in with other commitments.

There are also two major financial advantages to working from home. Overheads (rent, heat and light and so forth) are usually lower than for a business operating from commercial premises. This will improve your business's chance of being competitive and profitable. In addition, there are comparatively low start-up costs for many such businesses.

What are the disadvantages?

Working for yourself is nearly always arduous. You need to be motivated and disciplined and there is, generally, no one to take over if you are ill.

As well as productive work and getting sales, you will find that there is a lot of administrative work to be done: invoicing, filing, accounting, dealing with government agencies such as the Inland Revenue or Customs and Excise will all be your responsibility.

In addition, at least a small part of your home will have to be given over to the business and work will never seem far away. As with any business, there is the risk of failure.

Which business should I choose?

Choose a business that you like, find interesting and for which you have the necessary skills and aptitude. Be realistic. Do not be a cosmetics representative if you dislike perfume and are nervous about meeting people or a Web designer if you are no good at computers.

Once you have chosen a business, or have a shortlist of options, you will need to do some research to establish whether the business is viable and financially suitable. It is not a good idea to resign your full-time job only to discover, too late, that your business can only provide you with part-time earnings.

Where can I get ideas for a home-based business?

Keep your eyes and ears open and you will find plenty of ideas. Look in both national and local newspapers and business magazines such as *Start Your Business* and *Exchange & Mart*. When possible, attend business fairs such as the spring and autumn National Franchise Exhibitions. These sources will provide you with lots of ideas.

Another approach to generating ideas is self-appraisal. Examine your aptitudes, skills and hobbies. Jot these down on a piece of paper and this could trigger many suitable ideas.

For example, if your hobby is photography, there are many possible business activities linked to this. Besides the obvious suggestions of weddings and family portraits, you could consider the following:

- christenings;
- anniversaries;
- pet portraits;
- insurance work (providing a photographic or video record of valuables);
- providing portfolios (for bakers, florists, etc);

- production of items originating from photographs (badges, stickers, postcards);
- house photography;
- aerial photography.

Or are you experienced in computerised bookkeeping? The following might interest you:

- providing a computerised bookkeeping service to small businesses;
- training others in your skills;
- using your computer to provide services such as letter writing, CVs, and budgets;
- a consultancy service, setting up bookkeeping systems for new businesses.

A list of further ideas is given at the end of this chapter.

What types of home-based business are there to choose from?

The choice of business activities is wide and varied. They all, however, tend to fall into one of the three activities outlined below.

Providing a service

A service business can be set up with little capital outlay: for example, window cleaning, pet walking and house sitting.

You could choose to provide a service in a field in which you are already skilled or trained, such as aromatherapy, relaxation, secretarial work, bookkeeping, plumbing or carpentry.

Services that require greater capital outlay include computerised bookkeeping and carpet and upholstery cleaning.

PartyLite is the world's leading direct sales marketer of candles and candle accessories. Our products are sold through the home party plan by over 45,000 independent Consultants around the world.

PARTYLITE

PartyLite UK was established in 1996, and is one of the UK's fastest growing party plan companies. A member of the Direct Selling Association, the company's success lies in the combination of quality products and a realistic attitude towards business and income opportunities.

PartyLite's products are primarily candles – all of the finest quality available. The everyday market for candles and accessories has never been larger. PartyLite is committed to providing the answer for all candle requirements, all year round!

What Makes PartyLite a Special Opportunity?

- *Direct Selling Method:* Consultants sell to customers through in-home demonstrations - a time-honoured, efficient selling method, offering an enjoyable experience for customers and strong earning opportunity for Consultants.

- *Focus on Your Business:* PartyLite focuses on sales, sponsoring and leadership programmes to help Consultants grow their profitable business.

- *Quality Products:* Consultants have over 500 products to offer customers. PartyLite's candles and accessories are all crafted to ensure that customers are offered the best in quality and the latest, most exciting trends in candle decorating.

- *Profit Plan/Income:* Part of the reason behind PartyLite's growth and success is our Profit Plan. Consultants earn profits (income) by selling PartyLite products, by sharing the opportunity with others and teaching people sponsored into the business how to be successful.

- *Training:* PartyLite offers comprehensive support to Consultants via manuals, sales meetings and conferences, where Consultants and Leaders share successful strategies, keep updated with latest products and receive achievement recognition.

- *Incentives and Recognition:* We believe in encouraging success and recognising effort – with awards ranging from products, jewellery and monthly recognition, to trips to destinations such as Barcelona and Rome.

- *No Start-Up Costs:* PartyLite requires absolutely no cash investment to become a Consultant. A starter kit containing samples, sales brochures and order forms is supplied to Consultants when they hold a 'Starter Show' and schedule six more shows to begin their business. The Consultant begins earning Profits immediately, which increase with each new show – and there are no inventory or delivery requirements!

- *Customer Service:* PartyLite is committed to 100% customer satisfaction and backs this with a money-back guarantee.

When you become an independent Consultant with PartyLite UK, you join part of a growing team each with the opportunity to earn an income in their own time. Whether you are looking for the chance to supplement your income on a part-time basis or become a full time consultant, the option is yours.

You CAN have it all as an independent PartyLite Consultant!

For further information, please contact PartyLite UK:
215 Marsh Road, Pinner, Middlesex HA5 5NE (T) 020 8385 6600 (F) 020 8866 4800
info@uk.partylite.com www.partylite.com
Decorate your Home, Celebrate your Life, Illuminate your Spirit – with PartyLite

Manufacturing

At one extreme making things at home can be little more than an extension of a hobby such as knitting or sewing garments for friends and relatives. At the other end of the scale it can involve organising and coordinating the efforts of a number of outworkers.

It is wise to choose a product and manufacturing process with which you are familiar. Alternatively, ensure that adequate training is easily available. Most reputable firms providing machinery will arrange full training. Also, local colleges may run courses in your chosen discipline.

Home-operated machines can be bought that can print business cards, greetings cards or pens, or glaze photographs on to plates.

Selling

Many types of selling can be operated from home, including:

- party plan;
- multi-level marketing (MLM) or network marketing;
- door to door;
- telesales;
- Internet.

Party plan

Party plan selling involves selling goods to people at a gathering hosted in someone's home, not necessarily that of the manufacturer's agent.

The agent's role is to organise people to host such a party, to demonstrate the goods at the party, to take orders and to deliver the goods to the hostess for distribution. The agent receives a commission on the goods sold. Well-known party plan products include:

- Tupperware;
- clothes;

- jewellery;
- perfume.

Multi-level marketing or network marketing

Network marketing is essentially conventional direct selling combined with recruiting, helping and organising the efforts of others. You will, therefore, generate income from the sales you make and from those made by the people in your network who you organise.

Some such ventures have, in the past, given the technique a bad name, so do ensure that you join a bona fide business.

Popular goods for MLM selling have recently included household cleaners, electrical goods, books, and health and beauty products. Repeat orders products, such as cleaning fluid, usually do well in MLM since they are always in demand.

Door-to-door and telephone sales

Both door-to-door selling and telesales involve the selling of goods directly to the public and can be hard work. A number of hard-sell techniques have given this area a bad name too. So if you are trained by a direct sales company ensure that you are happy with the legality and ethics of their sales techniques.

Internet selling

Selling goods or services on the Internet readily lends itself to being operated as a home-based business, but it will require some initial outlay to get you up and running. You will need: an Internet-enabled computer, a domain name (unless you choose to operate through someone else's site), a Web hosting service and a Web site. If you wish to take payment online then you will also need a secure payments bureau or some additional programming to your Web site. The costs of these requirements can differ greatly, so do shop around. The more work you are prepared to do yourself, the cheaper the outlay will be, but be realistic about your capabilities or it will be very time consuming and frustrating.

Selling on the Internet allows your customers to order at a time that suits them, but to be successful, your site needs to be quick to download and easy to follow.

Is buying a franchise a good way to start a home-based business?

Yes, if you can find a suitable franchise. One of the most attractive aspects of franchising is its success rate, but this does come at a cost.

To run this type of business, the franchisee pays the business owner, the franchisor, for a licence. This will entitle you to use a trade name and proven business method. A good franchisor will, where appropriate, provide thorough training and support to the franchisee.

As with any other business opportunity you should carry out research to establish the viability of a franchise before parting with any money. The company providing the franchise should also be thoroughly reviewed, to ensure that it is financially sound. If the franchisor fails, so will you.

What facilities will I need?

This will depend upon the nature of your business. Working from home means that costs can generally be kept to a minimum. However, most businesses will need to consider transport, equipment and accommodation.

Transport

This is essential if you have to deliver to customers or collect from suppliers. It may be possible to use the family car, particularly if it is an estate or has a capacious boot. Do ensure that you are covered for such activities under your motor insurance policy.

For businesses that require you to move bulky items or large quantities of stock you may need to purchase a van or truck.

On the other hand, you may find that most of your delivery requirements can be adequately covered by the postal service, special delivery firms and public transport.

Equipment

General equipment requirements will include a telephone and an answering machine or a mobile phone, as customers will expect that you, or someone acting on your behalf, can take orders and answer queries at any time. The basic versions of this communication equipment are quite cheap. More expensive versions can have useful facilities such as e-mail, fax or remote message retrieval which allows telephone messages to be accessed while you are away from the answering machine. Also, a two-way conversation recording facility means a telephone conversation can be recorded. This is useful for taking orders. A typewriter, word processor or a computer will be necessary for neat presentation of letters and estimates. Also useful, but not essential for all businesses, are a fax machine and a photocopier. As an alternative to buying or leasing, these facilities are now available in the high streets of most towns.

A question often asked is whether a computer is an essential purchase for a home-based business. The short answer is 'no'. However, you may find it a useful purchase for accounts, budgets, letters and other business document preparation. As well as a potential timesaver the computer will give a more professional appearance to your documentation. Appropriate equipment and subscriptions can give you access to the Internet and e-mail (see Chapter 18, page 178). You may even be able to offer computer services to other small businesses, for a suitable fee, thus supplementing your main business income.

If you choose not to acquire a computer it is quite satisfactory to keep handwritten or typed accounts and records and invoices provided they are legible.

The Secrets of Home Fitness

Who doesn't dream of working towards, and maintaining a perfectly toned figure? Preferably without giving up anything in particular, being able to choose the most convenient time to exercise, and avoiding the hassle of going to the gym. And what's more, having great fun while working out! All this is now possible thanks to the enormous progress in home fitness technology.

Whatever your particular objective, the secret of success is not to rush things. You may have to prepare yourself mentally, but the important thing is to start off on the right foot by having a precise plan in mind and know what you want to achieve… to lose weight? To have a healthier lifestyle? It's your choice.

Setting yourself a goal – Everything can be done with time and a little application but your first goal must be a realistic one. The satisfaction you feel when you reach it will then encourage you to set more challenging targets.

ESTABLISHING A PROGRAMME – Check your diet, decide on the appropriate clothes and footwear, the best time of day for your workout, which exercises appeal most and how much time you'll dedicate to daily exercise.

CHOOSING THE RIGHT EQUIPMENT – which type of equipment will help you lose more body fat? Which type of equipment will give you an overall body workout?

A treadmill will help you achieve the highest body fat loss and as walking is the most natural way of moving, for both beginners and experts, the treadmill is the ideal piece of equipment to enable you to exercise in this way at home. As you increase your workouts, you will be able to move from walking to jogging by increasing inclines from 0-10% and speeds of up to 10mph. With shock absorbing Durasoft™ Cushioning on the NordicTrack range, the impact on joints is considerably reduced.

An elliptical machine is excellent for combining the benefits of a cycle, stepper, skier and a treadmill all in one with virtually no impact on joints. It allows you to target all the main muscles of the lower-body, will tone you and also burn fat. With upper body arms you can focus on your upper body major muscle groups which will not only make you stronger but also increase the amount of lean muscle mass, therefore burning even more fat.

There are many pieces of equipment to choose from, so for a full listing visit the NordicTrack website www.nordictrack.com/uk or call 0800 55 77 11 for your free brochure.

MOTIVATION – Why do you want physical exercise? List your reasons, keep them in mind and compare with the drawbacks of not working out. Remember with the NordicTrack range of products you can rely on iFIT.com and its training programmes for your motivation. You can even workout online with your own personal instructor!

To find out more about iFIT, visit www.ifit.com.

There is no magic formula to establish how much exercise a person needs. The most important thing to remember is a little is better than nothing. Generally speaking, it's best to start well below your maximum capability: begin slowly and gradually increase your efforts to achieve your goals.

Several studies show that the maximum benefit can be obtained by 200 minutes of moderate aerobic exercise a week. Exceeding this limit does not increase the benefit very much, (but the risk of hurting yourself does go up). On the other hand, 100 minutes exercise each week will give you approximately 90% of the maximum benefit, whereas 60 minutes will give you approximately 75%. Sixty minutes is only 15 minutes of moderate aerobic exercise four times a week!

Exercising three of four times a week is a reasonable frequency for aerobic exercise. If you alternate days, your body has time to recuperate. In any case you need at least one day's rest each week. Start with a few minutes and gradually increase up to around half an hour each session. Also, don't forget your warm up and cool down exercises; check your pulse rate by subtracting your age from the number 220 and obtain your maximum heart beat frequency level. Working out between 60 and 75% of your maximum heart rate will achieve maximum fat burn.

MAINTENANCE – If you've done all this, all the elements of your fitness plan are pretty much under control. The results you are looking for will come of their own accord and you can complete your programme. Physical exercise will become a habit, and a healthier way of life, all in the comfort of your own home gym.

The number 1 home working opportunity.

Can do all the hard work for Jamie, Lloyd, Nigella, Ainsley, Delia and You.

Home Sales Advisors

OTE £14k per annum

We all love gadgets that make life easier - and this is one machine that can genuinely improve the lives of thousands! Called a Thermomix - this is German innovation at its best. It can cook, mix, grate, whip, steam... in fact there's not much it can't do in the kitchen!

Every home should have one - and that's your aim! Working hours that fit perfectly around your existing commitments, you will use your personality, professionalism and ability to demonstrate products in the home to potential customers. Friendly and persuasive, you will convey your own enthusiasm for the product: 300,000 have been sold in Europe - so there's no hard sell!

If you're ambitious, there are significant opportunities to take your career further. So if you are looking for a new challenge, one where you can use your natural skills to earn excellent rewards - then join our nationwide team of Home Sales Advisors!

For an application form please call 0845 345 0722 or write to:

Vorwerk Thermomix UK, Vorwerk House,
Ashville Way, Wokingham RG41 2PL

Some products sell themselves.

Our best for your family

Vorwerk UK Thermomix

Everyone knows that one of the best ways to make money is through something you enjoy and if your passions lie in socializing and networking then a new kitchen utensil to hit the UK will give you the opportunity to go for gold.

The Thermomix from Vorwerk, the privately owned German group best known for its household appliances, has been tipped as the kitchen appliance which will revolutionise the British kitchen. Multi tasking is no problem for a Thermomix as it is the only utensil in the world to combine mixing and cooking. Said to replace up to 21 kitchen appliances it does everything from cooking, steaming, whisking, mixing to kneading. Already a must-have item in continental Europe, with 1 in 5 Italian kitchens blessed with one.

To be part of the Thermomix revolution,, all you have to do is use your social network and art of persuasion to encourage your friends and family to have a Thermomix demonstration in their homes. Once seen never forgotten you will have your audience transfixed as you transform the freshest of ingredients into the most scrumptious meals.

The demonstration can vary from a one to one or a handful of people – the decision is yours. Mouth watering dishes can be whipped up in an instant like watercress and almond soup, sorbets, ice creams or a full evening meal. Firm favourites they're always a winner.

Being part of the Thermomix network is certain to bring out the entrepreneurial side in you and the world really can be your oyster. Appealing to a wide audience, it is being snapped up by men and women who are moving towards fresh fast food made in the home in preference to chilled tray meals or take away meals from fast food outlets.

Vorwerk is a fast expanding Company in the UK and the introduction of the Thermomix offers marvelous career moves. Unique to the UK it presents a business opportunity that requires no start up investment and the strategic marketing plan offers two opportunities to earn. one from selling and the second from building your personal network.

From obtaining a solid income on a part-time basis to a fully professional career as a Group Manager, responsible for a personal organization the Thermomix offers one of the highest earning opportunities in the direct sales category. Representatives can expect to make up to £300 a week in their first year, with top Representatives making up to £100,000 by year 3.

Says XXX Thermomix Representative, "Demonstrating and selling the Thermomix is both financially and personally rewarding. People are always genuinely impressed when I demonstrate what the Thermomix can do and it really does change the way they cook and prepare food. For myself,, being my own boss and controlling my hours whilst earning a substantial second income for the household has been great – I recommend it to anyone."

If you think you've got what it takes and have the enthusiasm and perseverance to start your own business then the Thermomix is definitely your recipe to success.

All you have to do is ring 0845 345 0711 for more information.

Your particular business will determine more specifically your equipment requirements. For example, a business producing wedding videos will require high-quality video equipment, while a business requiring a high volume of correspondence would benefit from access to a word processor or PC and a high-quality printer.

Accommodation

Any home-based business will take up some space in your home. As a minimum you will require somewhere to produce your paperwork and a place to store it. A table and a small filing cabinet in a spare bedroom or in the kitchen will probably suffice. Bear in mind that business use of your principal private residence can affect your capital gains tax exemption. See page 146.

You may also require storage space for your stock, both finished articles and raw materials, and any equipment. If you are manufacturing products you will require space to do this. Ideally, you will be able to allocate a separate room. If this is not possible you may have to be well organised so that your business does not encroach on the domestic use of your home. Furthermore, with a home-based business, it can be more difficult to keep your stock and equipment secure from damage; children and pets have been known to wreak havoc.

More ideas for home-based businesses

- manufacture soft furnishings;
- be a children's entertainer;
- hire out equipment, for example bouncy castles for children's parties;
- become a social events organiser for parties, christenings, weddings and so forth;
- become a writer;
- become a consultant offering your skills and experience to other businesses;
- make gift baskets;

- run a catering business;
- become a beauty therapist;
- design and make jewellery;
- operate a mail order business, perhaps selling British-made goods abroad;
- design and make clothing;
- make clothing for people with special needs;
- frame pictures;
- engrave identity tags, dogs' discs, plates, etc;
- design or maintain gardens.

2 Researching the viability of a home-based business

What is a viable home-based business?

A business that generates adequate or more than adequate profits and cash flows for the owner. It is impossible to give a quantitative estimate for an adequate level of profits and cash flows as these will vary according to the nature of the business and the owner's personal financial requirements. When deciding what is sufficient for you and your enterprise, consider the following:

- what you will have to pay and when you will have to pay it;
- what you will receive and when you will receive it;
- what profit levels and cash flows similar business achieve;
- your personal financial commitments;
- how much income you could generate by using your resources elsewhere, for example by investing your capital in a bank or building society account and taking a full-time job;
- the likely number of hours you will be working;
- the advantages and disadvantages of working for yourself.

Why is viability important?

Without adequate profits and cash flows a business will fail and you will lose your investment of time and money. Both adequate profits and cash flows are necessary for a viable home-based business. If profits are not high enough there will be insufficient funds to reward yourself. If cash flows are too low you will not be able to meet the business debts as they fall due.

How do I know if a proposed home-based business is viable?

The simple answer is that you don't. You can never be certain, but you can take sensible steps to find out as much about the viability of your proposed business as possible.

One of the most important things to do is to prepare a cash flow statement or cash budget. This statement estimates the timing and amount of all the cash and cheques to be received and paid by your business. This should help you to decide if the cash flows are sufficient to pay the bills. It is worth emphasising that these statements are based on estimates (such as how many sales will be made and the level of costs) and are as reliable as the estimates upon which they are based. The preparation of cash flow statements is covered in more detail in Chapter 9.

To review the likely profitability of the business it is useful to prepare a budgeted profit and loss (P & L) account, which is covered in more detail in Chapter 12. The profit and loss account calculates profit by deducting costs from sales. Like the cash flow statement, the budgeted profit and loss account is based on estimates. Nevertheless, these two statements are different. The cash flow statement records any transaction that results in an increase or decrease in the business's cash funds, including cheques. The profit and loss account records sales and costs transactions that involve resources being depleted, for example:

Transaction	Effect
Stock is bought and paid for	This is recorded in the cash flow statement
The stock is sold on credit	The profit from this transaction will be reflected in the profit and loss account
The customer pays for the stock	This is reflected in the cash flow statement

Other things you can do to help gauge the viability of a home-based business include:

1. Find out all you can about the competition.
   - What prices do they charge?
   - What additional products and services do they offer?
   - Which areas do they cover?
   - Are there likely to be enough customers to support another business?

If any of the competition are limited companies you can obtain copies of their company reports, directors details and general company details from the Registrar of Companies.

For England and Wales contact:

> The Registrar of Companies
> Companies House
> Crown Way
> Maindy
> Cardiff CF4 3UZ
> Tel: 0870 333 3636
> Web site: www.companies-house.org.uk

For Scotland contact:

> The Registrar of Companies
> 37 Castle Terrace
> Edinburgh EH1 2EB
> Tel: 0870 333 3636

2. You may wish to carry out some basic market research about your potential customers. Discuss your ideas with other proprietors, potential customers, family, friends and neighbours. This should indicate whether there is a demand for your product or service and the price people are prepared to pay for it. When you are ready to carry out more detailed market research, refer to Chapter 5.
3. Try to find out as much as you can about the costs of your business. Ask suppliers for quotes or estimates, order limits and credit arrangements.
4. Carry out a few basic feasibility calculations. For example, is it physically possible to make the quantity of goods you need to sell to achieve a profit? This and other useful calculations are outlined on pages 25–28.

Is a going concern a viable option?

A going concern is a business that is already up and running. It is essential *not* to assume that a business is viable just being it is being sold as a going concern. Check it out for yourself.

What are the advantages of buying a going concern?

The main advantages are that:

● provided your investigations have been thorough, you should know what you are taking on;
● as the business is already up and running it can start earning you money as soon as you buy it;
● the teething problems of setting up a business have been dealt with.

What are the disadvantages of buying a going concern?

In the main these are that:

- the current owner will expect you to remunerate him or her for the above advantages as well as the assets of the business you are gaining;
- the business may not be exactly as you want it.

What information will a vendor of a going concern provide?

This will vary from business to business. As a minimum you should expect to see the balance sheet and the profit and loss account for the last few years. The balance sheet sets out the assets and liabilities of a business at a point in time, usually the end of the year. The profit and loss account details the revenues, expenditures and resultant profit or loss for a business, usually for a year. A more detailed explanation of these statements is given in Chapter 12.

Other information with which you may be provided includes budgets, order books, client lists, cash book or list of takings and a list of assets to be included in the sale (for example stock or machinery). The records will vary from business to business and from owner to owner.

Can I rely on the information provided by the vendor?

No. Treat this information with extreme caution. Most people are honest, but a few are not. Even an honest vendor may mislead you by omitting detrimental information. If you have ever bought or sold a house you will understand how this works. As a vendor, you volunteer the good points about your house but only disclose the drawbacks (perhaps you have noisy neighbours or leaky pipes) in response to a specific question.

Remember, just as with a house, a business vendor will present the business in as favourable a light as possible in order to obtain the best possible selling price.

If the going concern is a limited company, the balance sheets and profit and loss accounts may have been audited. This is a legally required independent check for limited companies which is evidenced by a signed audit report, a point which does give some credence to these reports. However, most companies with a turnover of not more than £1 million and with a balance sheet total of not more than £1.4 million are now exempt from compulsory audit. These limits are subject to change. Other than this, information provided by the vendor is unlikely to have been independently checked in any way. It is important that you keep this in mind.

How much should I pay for a going concern?

A going concern is worth however much someone is prepared to pay for it. When deciding how much you are prepared to pay, consider what you are getting for your money: stock, equipment, reputation, established produce or service, customer list. If possible, find out how much similar businesses are being sold for.

Chapter 19, pages 186–88, deals with some techniques used to value a home-based business for sale purposes. These techniques may be used by vendors and can be a useful guide to a purchaser.

Where will I find a going concern?

Try the following:

- local and national press;
- estate agents;
- business transfer agents (look in *Yellow Pages*);
- *Dalton's Weekly*, *Exchange & Mart* (both available from most newsagents);
- trade journals;
- local radio.

It may time time to find the right business, so do be patient. You will be investing a lot of time and money in your business so make sure you choose the right one.

Is it a good idea to buy a franchise?

Although you have to set up a franchise from scratch, provided you have carefully selected your franchisor you should be starting up with a proven business product or service.

A good franchisor will provide full and appropriate training for people it judges to be suitable franchisees. You should also be able to discuss the franchise with other franchisees. If you ask the right questions (make sure you write them down beforehand), this can be very informative.

The franchsior will usually require some financial remuneration from you. This can take various forms:

- You pay an initial investment to obtain start-up training and any necessary stock or equipment.
- You pay a monthly management charge. This will often cover ongoing training and administration.

- The product or service provided is obtained from the franchisor, who makes a profit on the transaction.
- You pay a proportion of your income from sales to the franchisor.

What information will a franchsior provide?

The franchisor should provide a forecast statement estimating how he or she expects the franchise to perform. This forecast is likely to outline expected cash flows, profits, assets and liabilities.

There will also be some explanatory background information with the forecast. This should explain the nature of the business, the product or service being provided, the current size of the business and expected growth, and the level of training and support to be provided.

The above information will help you to decide if the franchise is likely to suit you, but you will need to know more if you are to feel confident that it is a viable business proposition.

Ask the franchisor to provide the following:

- A copy of the franchise contract. This should cover such matters as the length of the franchise and any options to continue it after the initial period, remuneration to the franchisor and training and support to the franchisee.
- Copies of the franchisor's recent accounts.
- The franchisee's operations manual (this outlines how the franchise is to be operated).
- A map clearly outlining your territory.
- Details and the results of the market research carried out by the franchisor.
- Anything else you feel would help you to make your decision.

Will the franchisor provide reliable information?

Possibly, but it is best to assume not. When you are investigating a franchise you should be just as thorough as when investigating a business idea of your own, and as sceptical as when investigating a going concern.

In addition, I advise you to:

- Assess the viability of the franchisor. If he or she goes bust your franchise may be worthless.
- Speak to franchisees and, if you can, select them yourself.
- Check that the franchsior is a member of the British Franchise Association, whose members operate under a code of ethics. Contact the BFA at the address below to find out if they can offer any practical help.
- Where appropriate, check that the product has been patented and the business name registered. This will help to protect your business.
- Establish exactly what support and training is to be provided and how it is to be paid for.
- Find out whether the franchisor will be responsible for any advertising, what form it will take and who will be financially liable for it.
- Check exactly which exclusive area you are to be given and carry out your own market research to ensure that your catchment area will provide sufficient customers.

Review the contract thoroughly; does it outline clearly what is expected of the franchisee, what is expected of the franchisor and how each is to be remunerated? If you are considering signing a franchise contract I recommend that you take legal advice.

Where will I find a franchise?

In much the same places as a going concern (see page 22). Also, there are specialist magazines such as *Business Franchise and Franchise World*. If you are interested in a specific franchise contact the company's head office. The British Franchise Association may be able to help. Contact them at:

> Thames View
> Newtown Road
> Henley on Thames
> Oxfordshire RG9 1HG
> Tel: 01491 578050
> E-mail: mailroom@british-franchise.org.uk
> Web site: www.british-franchise.org.uk

Banks also offer impartial advice on franchising options.

How much should I pay for a viable franchise?

This is a very difficult area to advise on. In coming to your decision consider carefully what the franchisor is offering and how much money he or she requires in return. You will find it useful to look at other franchises to see how they compare.

How to calculate the viability of your business

A few basic calculations at the start of your investigations of a home-based business's viability could prove fruitful and time saving.

If a product is sold for £100 and all the costs (materials, advertising, travel, etc) of that product were £60, the profit would be £40.

$$\text{Sales} - \text{Costs} \quad = \text{Profit}$$
$$(\pounds100 - \pounds60 \quad = \pounds40)$$

This statement can be used to investigate the viability of a proposed business. If two of the items in this statement are known it is possible to calculate the third as we did above to establish that the profit was £40, knowing the sales and costs. Generally, it is more difficult to establish a sales figure and so here we will take this as the missing factor.

Establishing a sales figure

Estimate a profit using the following considerations:

- profit of similar businesses;
- profit you require before considering it worthwhile to run a home-based business.

Let us say your job earns you £10,000 gross salary and you must earn this amount before you can give up your job to run a business.

Next, estimate the costs of the business. Let us say that these are £2,000. In Chapter 9 you will learn how to estimate the costs of your business for yourself.

Now we are in a position to calculate the sales figure:

$$\text{Sales} \quad = \text{Costs} + \text{Profits}$$
$$= \pounds2,000 + \pounds10,000$$
$$\text{Sales} \quad = \pounds12,000$$

So, assuming costs are £2,000 and the profit required is £10,000, then sales needed to achieve this are £12,000.

Is the sales target achievable?

It will be difficult to be sure about this but the target total sales can be broken down to help this decision. The following three examples illustrate how this might be done.

Example 1

You are providing a service to your customers and have decided to charge them an hourly rate of £5. Thus the number of hours you need to charge your customers for is:

$$\frac{£12,000}{£5} = 2,400 \text{ hours}$$

Assuming four weeks' holiday and two weeks' sickness this works out in hours per week as:

$$\frac{2,400}{(52 - 4 - 2)} = 52 \text{ hours per week}$$

That is quite a long working week. Remember this is just for the time spent working for your customers. You will also have to spend time on the administration of your business.

Example 2

You are selling bought-in products to your customers. You are proposing to sell these at £10.

Therefore the number of items you need to sell is:

$$\frac{£12,000}{£10} = 1,200$$

Assuming the same holidays and sickness as for Example 1, this will require you to sell:

$$\frac{1,200}{(52 - 4 - 2)} = 26 \text{ items per week}$$

This is, assuming a five-day week, an average of approximately five items to be sold per day.

Example 3

You are making vases to sell to a local retailer who has agreed to pay £6 for each vase.

The number of vases you need to make and sell is:

$$\frac{£12,000}{£6} = 2,000$$

Assuming the same holiday and sickness as for Example 1, this will require you to make and sell:

$$\frac{2,000}{(52 - 4 - 2)} = 43 \text{ per week (approximately)}$$

For a five-day working week this is nearly nine vases each day. If you estimate that each vase takes you 1½ hours to make, then you will have to work 13½ hours each day just to make enough vases. On top of this there will be delivery and administration time, making a very long working day. Of course, you could try renegotiating with the retailer to increase your selling price.

3 *Starting up*

Who should I notify?

The following authorities should be notified of your intentions:

- The Local Authority Planning Officer for your area. It would be wise to do this well in advance of your first day of trading to ensure that there are no restrictions preventing you from operating as you wish.
- Contact your local Business Link before you commence trading. They may be able to offer you help and advice.
- The Inland Revenue. The local Tax Office will be in your telephone directory. They will advise you of any National Insurance (NI) contributions you are required to make.
- Customs and Excise. Chapter 15, page 154, will help you to decide whether you should register for VAT purposes. The current threshold for compulsory registration is an annual turnover in excess of £54,000. The amount is reviewed in each Budget.

What documents are required?

It is important that all the relevant documents are ready for the start-up of a business. If they are not available you may not record the transactions of the business accurately and deal with customers and suppliers efficiently.

As a minimum you are likely to require the following documents.

Sales invoice

A sales invoice is a document issued to customers showing certain information about the goods and services you are supplying. Before you organise sales invoices find out if you should register for VAT. If you do register you must include certain additional information on your sales invoice. A suggested format is given on page 99. Disclosure of business details on invoices is covered in Chapter 13.

Stationery

You will find it useful to have a stock of headed paper with your business details on it. The name of the sole trader, each partner, or the company must be given, together with an address for each person named where documents can be served. Other useful information, such as telephone and fax numbers, e-mail and Web addresses, should also be shown. Price lists, brochures, leaflets and business cards should all be ready for your business start-up as they will help to market the business and create sales.

What records should be kept?

The nature of the records you should keep is outlined in Chapters 10 and 11. I mention the subject here because it is very important to keep appropriate records as soon as you start up your business, particularly if you are spending money before you commence trading. It is all too easy to forget the details of early payments and receipts. If you forget to record any payments you will end up paying more tax. Any omission of receipts would result in an underpayment of tax. This could lead to an Inland Revenue investigation and fines.

It is also important to keep all business documents (for example, duplicates of sales invoices, purchase invoices, orders and any correspondence) so that you can verify all your transactions. If there is any dispute with the Inland Revenue the onus is on the taxpayer to prove his or her case.

What assets are required for a home-based business start-up?

These will vary from business to business.

Stocks

Consider your stock levels carefully. If you do not have adequate stocks of your product you may sell out and this can create a bad impression with your customers, as well as losing business. If you overstock, apart from having capital tied up unnecessarily, you may be left with obsolete, unsaleable stock. To help you estimate the level of stock, you need to consider the following:

- expected sales;
- finance available to buy stock;
- the nature of the stock (perishable, likely to become obsolete, seasonal, storage space required, time to replenish).

As an alternative to carrying large stock levels, consider taking orders by selling through a catalogue or carrying single items of each product for illustrative purposes. The drawback to this is that not all customers are prepared to wait for their goods.

Transport, equipment and accommodation

These are discussed in Chapter 1. You will need most of your business facilities ready for the start of trading. For example, it is futile to generate telephone interest in your business if the telephone is not answered, at least by an answer phone. However, do delay expenditure, where possible, until the business's outcome is more certain. For example, avoid buying additional transport if you are able to cope with the family car in the short term.

Finance

The level of finance you will require will depend upon:

- Opening stock levels.
- Transport, equipment and accommodation requirements.
- Opening advertising, selling and marketing costs.
- Other costs (for example telephone and stationery).
- Your desired remuneration, which will be dictated by your existing personal financial commitments. These may include mortgage repayments, pension, insurance, childcare or hire purchase repayments.

Other factors affecting the level of finance required are the credit periods allowed to customers and by suppliers. This dictates when your customers pay you and when you must pay your suppliers.

Unless you can arrange credit, all of the above will have to be paid for before the business generates any income.

Which form of business should I operate as?

The three main possibilities are:

- sole trader;
- partnership;
- private limited company.

Which form you choose will depend on the nature of your business and how you wish to operate.

What is a sole trader?

A business that operates with one owner or proprietor. It is, legally and administratively, the simplest form of business to use. If you wish to work as the sole boss of a relatively straightforward business, then operating as a sole trader may be your best option. Many home-based businesses operate as sole traders.

What are the advantages of being a sole trader?

Administratively, a sole-trader business is relatively easy to set up, run and wind up. To set up as a sole trader you simply notify the relevant agencies, as previously outlined, and start.

You may choose to employ people to work with you but ultimately you are responsible for all business decisions.

Unlike a limited company, there is no legal requirement for a sole trader to have an audit (this costs money but it is tax deductible). You do, however, need to provide accounting information for the Inland Revenue.

What are the disadvantages of being a sole trader?

There are two important disadvantages. The first should be considered very carefully.

If your home-based business runs into financial difficulties you become personally liable for any debts the business cannot pay. Your personal assets (house, car, shares) could be sold to meet these debts. Assets owned by your spouse are not affected unless they are specifically offered as security. Jointly owned property, often the family home, might have to be sold so that half the proceeds can be used to pay business debts. If your proposed home-based business is unlikely to run up large debts this need not be an important consideration for you.

Second, you are on your own, and so everything is down to you. You are the only source of capital and business experience.

What is a partnership?

A business that operates with more than one owner or proprietor. The joint owners are known as partners. A partnership may be an appropriate format for a home-based business if you wish to set up with someone else whom you respect and trust and who is essential to your operation.

What are the advantages of a partnership?

A partnership is similar to a sole trader in that it is still relatively easy to start, run and wind up and there is no legal requirement for an audit. To start, you simply notify the relevant bodies, prepare a partnership agreement and begin.

A partnership does have advantages over a sole trader in that all the partners can provide capital and business expertise, thus increasing the resources of the business.

What are the disadvantages of a partnership?

As with a sole trader, you are personally liable for the business debts. This will include any business debts incurred by your partner.

As you are working with other people on equal terms, differences of opinion may be difficult to deal with. To help avoid disputes, and resolve them if they occur, it is essential that a written partnership agreement is drawn up. It should address such matters as:

- responsibilities;
- remuneration and profit shares;
- working hours and holidays;
- decision making;
- resolving disputes;
- dissolving the partnership.

All partners are advised to take legal advice before signing a partnership agreement.

What is a limited company?

A limited company is a separate legal entity. In other words, it is separate from the owners (or shareholders) of the business. A limited company will be suitable for anyone who wishes to work on his or her own or with others.

The day-to-day running of the company is carried out by the directors of the company, who are appointed by the shareholders. Often, particularly with small businesses, the shareholders and directors are one and the same. A limited company can be formed using one shareholder, one director and a company secretary, providing that a sole director is not the secretary. There are no limits to the maximum number of shareholders or directors.

What are the advantages of a limited company?

The most important advantage of a limited company stems from the fact that the owners are seen as separate from the business. As a result the owners are not held liable for any of the debts of the business (unless they have entered into a separate agreement with a lender, such as a bank, or in certain cases of fraud). Personal assets are therefore protected from any business claims. By comparison, the other advantages are minor. They include:

● As a director of your company you will be an employee and so will be entitled to better benefits than if you had been self-employed.
● Administratively, it is quite straightforward to issue and re-sell shares to raise additional capital.
● Some people perceive a limited company as having higher status than a partnership or sole trader.

What are the disadvantages of a limited company?

Administratively, limited companies can be more expensive and more complicated to form, run and dissolve. To start a limited company you need either to consult a solicitor or to buy an 'off the shelf' company, as well as notifying the relevant agencies. Buying a ready-made company will save you administration time while setting up the business.

Furthermore, a limited company is required, by law, to prepare annual accounts in accordance with a legally prescribed format and to have them audited by a firm of auditors. You will have to pay for the audit; however, there is an exemption from audit where the annual turnover is not more than £1 million and the balance sheet total is not more than £1.4 million. These figures are subject to review.

As an employee of the company you will be subject to PAYE rather than enjoying some of the tax benefits available to the self-employed.

As a director you will have legal obligations to fulfil (these are outlined in Chapter 13, page 138).

What are the business's aims?

When starting out, it is important that you know what you want your business to achieve. Write down your aims and objectives so that you can monitor progress. Set financial and non-financial targets. Once these have been achieved you can set more. The aims and objectives of a business should be flexible and grow with the business.

4 *Raising business finance*

Where can I get finance?

Yourself

Most providers of finance will require some capital from the owner of the business; if you are prepared to risk your capital, they may risk some of theirs. The capital you provide could come from various sources:

- Cash from savings.
- Equipment for the business (for example a car or machinery).
- Cash from a personal loan.
- Cash from a remortgage of your home. Consider this option very carefully as your home could be repossessed if you fail to meet any repayments.
- Cash from the sale of personal assets (for example shares).

Banks

The banks are an obvious and generally good source of finance for the home-based business. When approaching your bank a good track record with your personal account should help in the negotiations for business finance. Most other banks will also be quite willing to listen to your proposal.

Family

Often the first person to offer financial help is a member of the family. Think very carefully before accepting such an offer. If the business gets into financial difficulties it could put a strain on relationships. Also, the lender might feel he or she has a right to become involved in the business.

If you do proceed with finance from within the family, put the arrangement on a formal basis by drawing up a written agreement. It is advisable for each party to see a solicitor to discuss the implications of the agreement. The agreement should address such matters as:

- the amount of the loan;
- length of the loan;
- interest rate payable;
- repayment dates;
- any security.

Government

There is a variety of schemes available from both central and local government. The most popular of these is the Business Start-up Scheme. To find out more about this programme, and whether you are eligible, contact your local Business Link.

The other main central government scheme is the Loan Guarantee Scheme which offers loans ranging from £5,000 to £100,000 for new firms to last for 2 to 10 years. The Department of Trade and Industry guarantees 70 per cent of the outstanding amount due to the lender. For firms that have been trading for more than two years loans of up to £250,000 are available with 85 per cent being guaranteed. To find out more about the scheme contact the Department of Trade and Industry.

Any schemes operated by local government will be specific to your area. To find out more contact your local authority.

Suppliers

Any credit period allowed by suppliers is a useful source of short-term finance. Unfortunately, many suppliers will not allow any credit until a business has a proven track record.

What are the different types of finance?

The main types are:

- loans;
- overdrafts;
- grants;
- capital;
- credit;
- hire purchase and leasing;
- factoring.

Loans

Loans provide medium- to long-term finance and therefore are a useful source of finance for the purchase of fixed assets such as machinery. The payment of interest and the repayment of the loan will all be agreed at the start of the loan period so that payments can be planned.

Often lenders will require some security for the loan. Frequently, the only asset entrepreneurs have is their home. If you are considering offering your home as security for a business loan take independent legal advice to make sure you are absolutely clear as to the possible consequences; if you default on repayments of the loan, your home could be repossessed.

Overdrafts

Overdrafts provide short-term, flexible finance and are, therefore, suitable for financing short-term assets such as stocks and debtors. On a day-to-day basis, provided you keep within your limit, you may borrow as much or as little as you wish, only paying interest on the amount borrowed. Overdrafts are usually agreed for a year, after which they are subject to review, and can be withdrawn without notice.

Grants

There are many types of grant available from many different organisations. Often the grant will be for a proportion of the costs, such as consultancy fees, or capital expenditure (for example, the purchase of machinery). The grant may come from a charity, local government, central government or the European Union.

Grants are not freely available to all businesses. The body offering the grant often has a specific purpose and will set criteria to achieve their purpose. Often bodies are concerned with:

- attracting business to an area;
- creating jobs;
- innovation and new technology.

Grants are usually of a one-off nature and as such are therefore suitable for non-recurring or infrequent expenditure such as equipment and consultancy fees.

Generally, grants cost nothing except the time and effort expended in finding out about them and the criteria to be met. Start by asking your local Business Link or your bank.

Capital

Capital is finance provided by the owner of a business. This will include any cash or assets provided by the owner and any retained profit. Retained profit is profit made by the business but not taken out by the owner as remuneration. Retaining profit helps to keep resources in the business and thus helps the finances. The capital of a limited company is called share capital and is provided by the owners buying shares in the company.

Capital provided by the owner is usually long term and is therefore suitable for the purchase of long-term assets such as equipment, machinery and motor vehicles.

Capital is limited to the amount the owner(s) can personally provide. There is no requirement to pay any interest on capital, although where partners provide different levels of capital, it may be equitable to do so. The owners of a limited company will expect to be paid a dividend but this is their share of the profits, not a payment of interest.

Credit

Credit enables a business to enjoy the benefits of goods or services before paying for them. It will be given free of charge for an agreed period, usually 30 days. Exercise caution, because some supplies charge interest if you are late with a payment, and the supplier is at liberty to withdraw a credit facility at short notice.

Credit is thus a useful, cheap source of finance which should be used wherever possible. Even if the credit is not required it can be used to keep business funds in interest-earning accounts. Credit can often be obtained from suppliers once you have proved yourself to be a reliable customer.

Hire purchase and leasing

Hire purchase is a form of credit purchase for which the customer pays a relatively high rate of interest. On the other hand, hire purchase is comparatively straightforward to obtain. This is partly because if you default on your repayments the vendor is entitled to repossess the goods. Hire purchase agreements are suitable for purchasing long-term assets, such as machinery.

Leasing is similar to renting except that the responsibility for maintaining the asset lies with the lessee. Usually the lessee will be obliged to lease for a minimum period. At the end of the lease period the lessee will usually have an option to buy the asset, such as a car or photocopier.

Factoring

For a fee, usually a percentage of sales, a factoring service will advance a proportion of the business's credit sales, the balance usually to be paid when the customer pays. This reduces the amount required to finance credit sales. The factoring service may refuse some customers or refuse to accept sales made to them over a certain limit.

Banks can also provide information and more information can be obtained from:

> Factors and Discounters Association
> 2nd Floor, Boston House
> The Little Green
> Richmond
> Surrey
> Tel: 020 8332 9955
> Web site: www.factors.org.uk

When will I need finance?

It is necessary to constantly review the business's finances but there are three situations that require particular consideration.

Start-up

It is important to choose appropriate finance so that the balance between your long-term and short-term finance reflects the balance between your long-term and short-term needs.

Expansion

If you are considering expanding your business it is likely that it is a successful business. Unfortunately, many businesses have failed when attempting to expand. This is often due to expanding too quickly or with too little finance. Expansion of any kind will require additional resources which have to be financed and planned for.

Completion of a major order

This is effectively a temporary expansion of the business. It will require additional finance but only for the duration of the order.

Where can I go for business advice?

The banks are the obvious choice and offer support through a wide range of finance schemes. Accountants should also offer sound advice. Your local Business Link, the Department of Trade and Industry and the Department for Employment and Skills may also be able to help.

How should I approach a lender for finance?

Before you approach any lender it is essential that you are well prepared. The lender will expect to see a professional, competent, knowledgeable, committed proprietor with a coherent and realistic business plan (see below). These will be the main factors on which the lender will base a decision. It is, therefore, essential that both you and your business plan are well prepared and presented.

The business plan

The business plan has two main uses. It is a very important document that helps the owner to plan and control his or her business in the present and for the future.

The business plan is also used to raise finance. Its aim is to inform the lender about the proposed business venture. In particular the lender will want to know:

- Is the business viable?
- How much is being borrowed?
- What type of finance is required?
- Is the business capable of repaying the borrowings and paying any charges and interest?
- What security is being offered?
- How much capital is the owner contributing?

So the business plan is likely to contain the following headings:

- *Background information*. Background information should inform the lender of the nature of the business, its location, size, methods of selling and explain any manufacturing process involved.
- *Marketing information*. This section needs to convince the lender that you have a viable product or service that can achieve a reasonable level of sales.
- *Financial information*. This will include a cash flow forecast, together with the assumptions made in preparing it, and is the subject of Chapter 9.
- *Finance*. This will outline borrowing requirements, repayment details, charges and capital introduced.
- *Owners and senior management*. The skills, knowledge and experience of key personnel should be given.

You should spend time on, and pay care and attention to, the business plan, making sure that it is clear, concise and well presented. It should be typed or word-processed. You may wish to seek professional advice from an experienced accountant, consultant or your local Business Link.

Presenting yourself

It is essential that you are fully conversant with the content of your business plan and your proposed business. The lender will need to have confidence in you as well as your business. It would be advisable to rehearse the meeting with your prospective lender with a friend or colleague. You might also consider approaching your preferred lender after you have had practice meetings with other lenders. This should ensure that you are well prepared.

5 *Marketing*

What is marketing?

Marketing is about finding out what the customer wants or needs and then providing it. Marketing is important to the home-based business which, with its limited resources, is particularly vulnerable to marketing errors. Customers buy what they want, not what you think they want, so you should ensure that you know what they want and can therefore provide it.

Many people consider marketing to be an avoidable expense, but before you dismiss it outright consider carefully the costs of business failure. It would be expensive and time consuming to set up business as a beautician in a purpose-built extension to your home, only to find that many of your customers would prefer to relax in the comfort of their own homes.

What is market research?

Market research is the investigative work carried out to generate marketing information. Market research techniques include:

- questionnaires;
- reviewing information on market trends which is in the public domain;

What if

you could

build your own business

around the world's

best-selling

weight-control

products?

For over 20 years, Herbalife's nature-inspired products have helped millions of people lose weight, support your health and enjoy life to the fullest. The Herbalife business offers you a unique opportunity to share these fantastic products with others by running a business from your own home.

Having a business of your own couldn't be more fun or more rewarding.

- informal discussions;
- observation;
- collating internal information.

Questionnaires

If a questionnaire asks precise, appropriate questions it will provide useful information direct from potential customers. A simple questionnaire can be prepared and implemented by anyone. Take care to set out your research objectives and then check that your questionnaire meets these objectives. Remember to include appropriate interviewee details such as age, sex, transport and distance travelled. Record all answers: do not rely on memory.

If the questionnaire is to be of value it is important to interview appropriate people. For example, it is of little value to question people about a house-sitting service if they are neither a home owner nor a tenant.

When the questionnaire relates to a product it may be beneficial to show the interviewee the product itself. This is more likely to generate interest and thus informative responses.

The questionnaire could be implemented by post or over the telephone. The costs of these methods could be prohibitive to a small business since the hit rate, particularly for a postal questionnaire, could be low.

Reviewing public information

Much of the information required for marketing purposes is already publicly available, for example:

- Commercial telephone directories such as *Yellow Pages* and *Thomson* will provide details of local competition.
- Trade directories: *Kelly's Industrial Directory*, *Dun and Bradstreet Directories* and others give information on various types of business.

- Local press: details of local competition.
- New product directories: information on new products.
- Trade journals: details of competition and innovation.
- *Census County Report*: analysis of the population, for example by age and sex.
- *Family Expenditure Survey*: income and expenditure information.
- Business monitors: sales, profit and expenses for different types and sizes of business.
- The Internet contains a great deal of information, such as competitors' prices, products and services, but it can take time to access the precise information you are after.

Since most of the above can be found at a nearby library there is no excuse for not carrying out market research. A selection of useful contact addresses is given at the end of this chapter.

When looking at any public information it is important to consider how recent it is. For instance, statistics on the age of a population can rapidly become out of date. If you are using monetary data this can be updated by using the retail price index (RPI).

The RPI is a measure of inflation obtained by calculating the changes in the average price of a collection of goods and services. The following example illustrates how the RPI can be used to update monetary information. Assume that the average amount spent on clothing per person is £500 for 2001, the retail price index at the end of 2001 is 100 and at the end of 2002 is 110. This means prices have increased by 10 per cent. A reasonable estimate of the amount spent on clothing per person for 2002 would therefore be £550 (£500 + (£500 × 10%)).

Informal discussions
A great deal of information can be ascertained by simply talking and listening to people. Talk to other business proprietors, potential and existing customers, family and friends; most people will be only too pleased to give you their opinions.

Observation

Where possible, studying current and potential customers and the competition can reveal useful marketing information. For example, observation of a local craft shop can provide a craft worker with information on customer demand.

Collating internal information

A lot of marketing information can be generated within your own business. One of the advantages of the home-based business is that the owner is likely to be in close contact with many customers, and thus able to identify their requirements. If you have staff remember that they can gain useful knowledge of customers and competitors. You will also have records of sales, stocks, orders and enquiries; a little analysis of this will generate useful marketing information, for example sales volumes for each product, and any unsatisfied demand.

You, too, will accumulate a great deal of knowledge – use it to improve the products or services you offer your customers.

Why is market research important?

Market research tries to answer many of the questions you will have already asked yourself:

- Who will be your customers?
- What will they buy?
- How much will they buy?
- How much are they prepared to pay?
- Where do they want to buy?
- What sort of service do they expect?
- What is the competition doing?

Although you can never get precise answers to your questions, thorough market research should provide sufficient information to enable you to make informed decisions.

The information provided by market research will greatly enhance the chances of a business meeting the customers' requirements. It is vital to get it right first time. Mistakes are costly.

It is often the anticipation of a personal high standard of service that leads customers to use home-based businesses, so be ready to provide them with what they want.

How can market research information best be used?

Once you have completed your market research you should have the answers to some fundamental questions, such as who your customers are likely to be and what the competition is doing. A great deal of time and energy will have been expended so it is important to act on your findings. For example, you may find that your original idea for a home-based business is not viable – perhaps because there are already too many competitors. You may, therefore, look at other possible opportunities, or perhaps the marketing information identified a gap in the market upon which you can capitalise.

The information you have gathered may highlight ways in which you can differentiate your services from those of a competitor. As an example, a word-processing business could offer free duplicates of all documents. Perhaps the market for computerised bookkeeping services is full but your market research indicates that offering to include taxation, VAT and budgeting would encourage many customers to use your services.

The package you offer to customers will affect the price they are prepared to pay and the likelihood of their becoming regular customers. Do your customers require quality, reliability, after-sales service and convenience? Do they expect to pay an 'all in' price or do they prefer to pay for items separately?

Public statistics, such as those provided in census reports and the

Family Expenditure Surveys, can be used to estimate the potential market and thus possible levels of sales.

Used properly, market research information can be used to tune your business accurately to the requirements of your customers.

Sources of marketing information

Local library (you may need to visit the nearest business library). You can discuss your requirements with the librarian who will be able to offer help and advice.

The following organisations charge a fee for their services to companies that take part in comparisons.

The Centre for Inter-firm Comparison provides information which helps companies to assess and improve their performance, and can be contacted at:

> 32 St Thomas Street
> Winchester
> Hampshire SO23 9HJ
> Tel: 01962 844144

Credit information is available from:

> Dun & Bradstreet Report Line
> Holmers Farm Way
> High Wycombe
> Buckinghamshire
> HP12 4UL
> Tel: 01494 423242
> Web site: www.dnb.com

The *Annual Abstract of Statistics* gives 10 years' worth of statistics, enabling trends to be identified. It is published by:

The Office for National Statistics
Cardiff Road
Newport NP10 8XG
Tel: 0845 601 3034
E-mail: info@statistics.gov.uk
Web site: www.statistics.gov.uk

Business Briefings, a magazine which monitors business news and statistics is produced by:

The British Chambers of Commerce
Manning House
22 Carlisle Place
London SW1P 1JA
Tel: 020 7565 2000
E-mail: administrator@britishchambers.org.uk
Web site: www.britishchambers.org.uk

All data published by the Business Statistical Office, including manufacturing, economic and financial statistics, is obtainable from The Office for National Statistics (address given above).

The Market Research Society produces a directory that provides details of organisations offering market research services and can be contacted at:

The Market Research Society
15 Northburgh Street
London EC1V 0JR
Tel: 020 7490 4911

6 *Selling products and services*

How can sales be increased?

Sales are vital to a business's success. In general, the higher the level of sales the higher the profit. Unfortunately, the level of sales achieveable by a home-based business may be limited by lack of facilities such as storage space. A certain level of sales must be achieved in order to break even. Fortunately for home-based businesses, because of their lower overheads, the break-even level of sales can be relatively low.

Additional sales will come either from existing customers or from new customers. It can be very difficult to increase sales levels, particularly where there is strong competition. Remember that any discounts or price cuts, to increase sales, will reduce the profit per unit, although the additional units sold may more than compensate.

Existing customers

Home-based businesses offering a personal service are likely to be in a strong position to generate additional sales from existing customers:

- use your customer knowledge to offer other suitable products;

DIRECT SELLING
– a business opportunity for everyone

Richard Berry

Director, Direct Selling Association

Whatever happens to the economy in the coming year, economic experts throughout Europe and North America agree on one thing. It is that:

- The prospects of lifetime salaried employment are rapidly diminishing;
- Creating wealth from manufacturing will continue to decline in favour of businesses supplying services;
- Big businesses devoted to supplying services will continue to look for ways of using technology to replace humans;
- The average number of people employed in all businesses will continue to decline;
- Future prosperity will depend on new very small businesses and on self employment.

Direct selling is, today, Europe's largest provider of the independent earnings opportunities that will be needed in every Member State. Providing encouragement and reducing the obstacles to self employment is a top UK government priority. That is why the Prime Minister, Tony Blair, recorded a message of support last year to the Direct Selling Association and to all those who have taken the initiative to start their own small business with DSA member companies.

Starting any type of new business is tough, risky and needs start up capital. You may have a great idea, but there is no guarantee that it will work in practice – and then there is the challenge of selecting the most cost effective way of finding customers. Franchise opportunities, with a proven business format, do help to reduce the risk element – but they still need capital, and usually quite a lot.

A flexible and proven business opportunity, requiring only a modest investment in a business kit and which can be started on a part time basis, is what direct selling is all about – and is why, in the UK alone, almost half a million people a year are taking up these opportunities. Many of today's entrepreneurs gained their first experience of business with a direct selling company. It is also why direct selling is now recognised as making such a valuable contribution to the economy.

For anyone considering which of the many business opportunities to take up, the marketing of a service also has some obvious appeals. There is no need to buy and keep stocks of goods and none of the hassle involved in delivering orders. However, for all the benefits, selling an intangible service is not for everyone. Just talk to anyone who tried selling life insurance! You cannot see, feel or sense the aroma of a service. Getting the message across needs communication skills and, frequently, considerable selling skills. Happily however, direct selling businesses today offer something for everyone. In looking for a business that suits you there are some golden rules to follow.

The first is to be assured that the product or service is something that appeals to you. If it does, and if you think that the selling price to a consumer is fair and reasonable, then it will not make too many demands on your selling skills. You will find that your enthusiasm will do the selling for you. A personal endorsement is far more powerful, and honest, than a sales pitch.

The second is particularly relevant to Multi Level Marketing (MLM) businesses. It is to forget the idea that the prospect of high commissions and bonuses can offset any personal doubts you may have about the product. At the end of the day, a 'rich' sales plan with a product that is difficult to sell will not serve you as well as more modest commissions earned from offering a product you like, with a proven selling method.

The third is not to be seduced by the prospect of getting in on the 'ground floor' at the launch of a new business in the UK – even if it has enjoyed spectacular successes in other markets. If it satisfies the first two rules, go for it, if it doesn't, forget it ! Many of the most outstanding personal success stories in direct selling and network marketing come from those who have quite recently joined a good, sound business that has been established here for twenty years or more. No more than one in six of the UK's adult population have ever had any experience of a direct selling business, so the remaining market is huge.

The fourth is to be very wary of any presentation that promises 'passive' earnings. By that I mean the prospect of earnings that will come constantly and automatically from every customer you sign up to a service. We live in a competitive world and customer loyalty can never be guaranteed. Of course, loyalty can be achieved, but it has to be earned - and that means constantly looking after your customers. This is what every business has to do.

Finally, check that the business that appeals to you does comply with UK law. If it is a DSA member, that is one useful safeguard - as the DSA demands and checks that compliance. With the increasing number of businesses now being promoted, worldwide, on the internet, this check is becoming more and more important. Just because a business plan, a form of contract or a commitment to an initial payment, is acceptable in the US, it is no guarantee that it is acceptable in the UK. As it happens, UK legal requirements are quite reasonable but the DTI does demand strict legal compliance. For information on the DSA, its member companies and its codes of practice, visit the DSA website www.dsa.org.uk

As the direct selling channel continues to achieve record sales, just remember this. Direct selling is, today, the UK's largest provider of independent earnings opportunities. The reason is simple, the cost of starting such a business is so little compared with the financial rewards it can yield.

- build up a good working relationship;
- consider offering bulk discounts;
- inform the customer of any new product or service.

A satisfied customer will be a good source of repeat orders and may generate new business by recommending your services to others.

New customers

To save time and money it is important to target potential customers. Follow up all enquiries. After all, these are people sufficiently interested in your services to have contacted you. However, you will only be able to follow up those leads if you have a record of them; so make sure you write down details of all business enquiries.

Ask existing customers if they know of others who might be interested in your products.

Where you have no new leads or referrals to pursue, try to narrow down your list of other possibilities. This may be from your mailing list or advertising catchment area. For example, offer sign-writing services to new businesses requiring signs or established ones requiring an update. If you offer a delivery service contact those most likely to use it: customers without transport or those who live out of town.

How do I sell to customers?

Many people are nervous about selling, but it is vital to your business and must be effective. If you are inexperienced, consider the sales courses provided by some colleges or other training institutions. Some general tips are:

- use your market information to help you emphasise the relevant points of your goods and services;
- know what you are selling;

- remember to listen;
- practise telephone sales, presentations, demonstrations and negotiations.

When approaching customers the first step is to make an appointment. Be prepared to:

- explain concisely what you are offering and why it is worthy of consideration;
- provide positive responses to any likely objections;
- be flexible over appointment times;
- keep a record of all relevant points.

Be ready for your appointment. Rehearse what you wish to say. This will include the relative merits of your products and services, the good reputation of your firm and any references you are proposing to give. Try to anticipate likely objections and be ready with a suitable response. Ensure that equipment you may need is in working order.

Be punctual, appropriately dressed, polite, calm and, above all, concise. Do not waste your potential customer's time.

Once you have a verbal order it is important to follow this up to ensure that a sale results. Prepare a written order and send a copy to the customer to make sure there has been no misunderstanding.

Remember to be well rehearsed and never apply too much pressure, as this can be counterproductive.

What sales methods are available to the home-based business?

Almost all methods of selling are suitable. However, by definition, this will exclude selling from your own business premises. Choose from the following:

- sell to retail outlets;

- sell to warehouses;
- sell direct to the public using party plan, door-to-door, networking, mail order, agents and the Internet.

Party plan, telesales, door to door networking, and the Internet are discussed in Chapter 1 on pages 6–7.

Selling to retail outlets

This is an excellent way for the home-based business to enjoy the volume of sales achievable in a retail outlet without taking any of the associated financial risks. Ask the retailer to buy your stock outright, take your stock on a sale or return basis or to rent space in the shop to you. The latter is likely to appeal to retailers as it will increase their range of stock at no extra cost and at the same time generate additional income.

Selling to warehouse outlets

This is similar to selling to retail outlets. The advantage with a warehouse is that your products are likely to reach a wider range of retailers and customers. The main disadvantage is that you will have no control over whoever sells your goods to the public and so cannot influence the way in which your products are sold.

Mail order

For the right kind of product, mail order can be the ideal selling method for the home-based business. Goods can be produced to order, payment can be received (and banked and cleared) before they are despatched. Storage problems can be reduced because goods can be despatched as soon as they are ready. The main drawback to mail order is the cost of advertising and promotion.

Before opting to use mail order make sure that your market research indicates that your products can be successfully sold this way. A good range of products will be needed to keep customers coming back.

Selling via an agent

Agents work for themselves selling products for commission. You should find out whether they sell competing products. As you will have little direct control over their activities, it may be wise to draw up a written agreement.

Which sales methods should I use?

This will depend upon you, your business and your finances. Take note of the marketing information you have generated: are certain methods preferred by your target market? Which methods suit you? Which methods generate the greater profits?

If you are not keen to do the selling yourself consider using a different method – using a sales representative, an agent, a retail outlet, warehouse or the Internet. These alternatives will reduce your work load, although you will lose some control over how your products or services are presented to the customer, and getting feedback on your customers' reactions will be more difficult. It is also likely to increase your costs or reduce your profit per unit because sales representatives and agents will require remuneration for their efforts, and retail outlets and warehouses may require commission or insist on buying at a lower, trade price.

Limited finances may also influence your choice of selling methods. A retail or warehouse outlet will probably require stock to be delivered in batches, and payment to you will be on a sale or return basis at the end of the month of sale. This will require a significant level of finance. Other methods of selling more easily lend themselves to payment with order.

What about selling a service?

Selling a service can be more difficult than selling a product, especially for a home-based business. Where there is no product to see, premises become a more prominent sales persuader. To help alleviate this problem:

- Show customers any letters of recommendation, complimentary letters or other documentary evidence (for example, 'before and after' photographs).
- Give the names and addresses of satisfied customers who have agreed to act as references.
- Explain the qualifications and experience that make you an appropriate person to provide the service.
- Clearly describe the service you provide and how it differs from other similar services.

How can I promote my home-based business?

Promotion is essential to every business. If consumers do not know what you are selling, or how to buy from you, they are unlikely to become your customers.

Home-based businesses are at a disadvantage because there are no business premises to capture passing trade, but as there are numerous other promotional techniques available, this should be only a minor disadvantage.

The most important and effective of these methods is personal recommendation passed by word of mouth. A satisfied customer is a very persuasive sales weapon.

Remember, every contact with a potential or existing customer is a chance to promote your business, its products and services. It is consequently important that both you and your staff are courteous and helpful at all times. Make sure that the telephone is answered in a polite and informative way so that customers are aware that they have the correct number and know to whom they are speaking. Make sure that all orders and sales are processed promptly and efficiently, and if problems arise keep the customer informed. All written communications should be professional and accurate. Along with personal recommendation, efficiency and courtesy are powerful promotional tools.

Such methods will take time to generate a viable level of sales. Below are some methods that can be used to more immediate effect.

Trade magazines

Where a suitable trade magazine is available it is likely to provide access to some target customers. National trade magazines can be invaluable to the home-based business that wishes to sell throughout the UK, or even internationally, but they are unlikely to reach all target customers.

Leaflets

These can be delivered to homes, left in shops and public buildings or handed out in a local shopping centre. It may be necessary to obtain permission for distributions which are not to homes. In appropriate circumstances leaflets can be a very useful way of reaching target customers; for example, leaflets advertising a taxi service could be delivered to homes which do not have a nearby supermarket.

The main problem with leaflets is their distribution. The most reliable delivery service is yourself, but this is time consuming. Businesses specialising in leaflet distribution can be found in the *Yellow Pages* under 'Circular and Sample Distributors'. Try to use a firm that has been personally recommended. Milkmen, the post office and local newsagents are also likely to offer this service.

Another drawback with leaflets is that they are often quickly discarded. Give people a reason to keep them; for instance, allow a discount if the customer presents the leaflet.

Newspaper advertising

Newspapers are likely to reach a wider audience (the paper will provide you with circulation figures), though only some of its readers will be in your target market. Beware of free newspapers as these may not even be read before they are thrown away.

If possible, insist on a suitable position for your advertisement, such as health and beauty services on the women's page.

Business directories

These include the *Yellow Pages* and the *Thomson Directory*. There may also be local directories in your area. Consider carefully which type of entry is most appropriate. A larger box entry is most likely to catch the eye but will be more expensive. If there is little or no competition in the directory for your business activity a standard entry may be quite sufficient.

Local radio

The local radio will reach a wide variety of people so it is important to advertise when your target market is most likely to be listening, for example, garden design and gardening services shortly before or after gardening programmes.

Other

Other possibilities include:

- Shop windows. Try to attract attention and select a prominent position on the board.
- Business cards.
- Posters at colleges, libraries and schools.
- The Internet.
- Packaging and carrier bags.
- Exterior of your business vehicle. This is doubly useful if you are offering a mobile or delivery service.
- Fairs and craft shows.

When preparing an advertisement consider the following:

- Employ a copywriter and a designer.
- Include all relevant information.
- Use persuasive words such as 'guarantee', 'proven', safety', 'health', 'easy', 'new', 'save' and 'money'.
- Use colour photographs, graphics and position to make your advertisement eye catching.
- Try to generate action by offering a discount or free trial for a limited period or while stocks last.

When choosing a method of promotion think about cost, which methods are most likely to reach your target market, how many potential customers will be reached, and how durable the advertising is.

Don't forget that promotion should not be approached as a series of isolated exercises but should be carried out as a single, cohesive, continuous campaign.

7 *How to price products and services*

How much should I charge?

There is no easy answer to this vital question. The price you charge will be based on a number of factors, one of which will be gut feeling. Others include:

- supply and demand;
- the competition;
- discounts;
- resources;
- VAT;
- the future;
- market and research information;
- cost and profit.

Why are competitors and supply and demand relevant?

If you are fortunate enough to be offering a unique products there will be no competition. In these circumstance you may well be able to demand a high price: but be warned, this will attract competition.

Where there is already competition, find out how much they are charging. To attract customers you will need to set a competitive price, unless your product is clearly superior.

A market where supply is greater than demand will be very cut-throat, and you will be wiser not to get involved.

Should discounts be offered?

Many home-based businesses, because of resource limitations, aim for low-volume, high-profit sales. In this situation it may not be necessary to offer discounts, although they can be useful to attract the larger-volume customer or improve sales during quiet periods. The discount you offer will depend on how badly you need the business and how big a discount your competitors are offering.

How can resources affect prices?

Many home-based businesses will encounter resource limitations. In particular, storage or work space may be at a premium. It is pointless to set prices to generate a level of sales that cannot be effectively dealt with.

What about value added tax (VAT)?

If you are registered for VAT (see Chapter 15) you are obliged to charge your customers VAT. The rates are 17½ per cent for standard rate goods and nil for zero rated. The VAT is payable to Customs and Excise. If your customers are also registered for VAT and the goods or services you supply are used in the furtherance of their businesses, they will be able to reclaim any VAT you have charged. They will, therefore, pay the same for your goods and services whether you are registered for VAT or not.

However, customers not registered for VAT will have to pay 17½ per cent (the rate is subject to change by government) more for your standard rate goods and services if you are registered. The majority of goods and services are standard rate.

What should the future pricing policy be?

Prices should be continually reviewed to keep abreast of any changes. Prices may be set low in the short term to help generate business. Once custom has been built up, prices may be increased.

How does market research help pricing?

Market research will provide useful information about what your customers want and how much they are willing to pay.

Appropriate market research can indicate:

- how much, approximately, customers are prepared to pay;
- which items customers wish to pay for separately and those which they consider inclusive;
- whether clients are prepared to pay more or less (than to competitors) for your goods and services.

What influence do costs and profits have on prices?

To make a profit you will need to sell your goods and services at a higher price than they cost you. Costs plus desired profit can, therefore, be a useful pricing yardstick.

How can costs and profits provide a pricing yardstick?

Calculations for pricing range from the simple to the near impossible. The degree of difficulty will depend upon:

- the nature of the home-based business;
- how precise the calculations are.

It is best to simplify the calculation as much as possible. The reasons for this are that:

- it saves time;
- it is simpler to understand and therefore less prone to error;
- the price will be based on estimates and assumptions and is therefore, at best, only an approximation;
- other factors will need to be considered as well.

Pricing a product

The estimated costs of a gift basket business for the year are shown in Table 7.1.

The level of turnover shown must be derived from the sale of 100 baskets, and so each basket must be sold for about £51. Now compare this price with that of competitors and consider your market research information.

Pricing a service

When providing a service it is often a good working method to establish a rate per hour. Customers can then be charged for the hours worked. This can also be useful for providing quotes.

The estimated annual costs of a computerised bookkeeping service are shown in Table 7.2.

Table 7.1 Estimated costs of a gift basket business

		£
Baskets	100 @ £1 each	100
Gifts	100 @ £2 each	200
	100 @ £3 each	300
	100 @ £10 each	1,000
Decorations for 100 baskets		70
Postage and packaging 100 @ £5		500
Telephone and sundries for the year		320
Sales commission 100 @ £1.50 each		150
Total costs		2,640
Desired profit		
(based on alternative part-time work)		2,500
Total sales required		5,140

Table 7.2 Estimated annual costs of a computerised bookkeeping service

	£
Lease of computer and software	1,000
Stationery, postage and telephone	450
Advertising	350
Desired profit	
(based on alternative full-time employment)	10,000
Total sales required	11,800

When estimating the number of hours you expect to work for customers, take account of holidays, illness, non-productive time (for example preparing your own accounts) and idle time when there is no work.

The number of hours you can expect to work for customers might look something like Table 7.3.

Table 7.3 Hours spent working for customers

	Weeks
Total in year	52
Less holidays	4
Illness	2
Non-productive time	2
Idle time	4
Chargeable weeks	40

If we assume a working week of 35 hours, you will work a total of 1,400 hours for clients. Thus the rate per hour is approximately £8.50 (11,800 ÷ 1,400). The calculations in both examples are only valid if all the assumptions and estimates are accurate. Profits will be reduced if:

- you sell fewer hours or products;
- your costs are higher;
- your selling price is lower.

Profits will be increased if:

- you sell more hours or products;
- your costs are lower;
- your selling price is higher.

The above examples are useful if the products or services you are providing are the same or of a similar nature and value.

A more detailed situation

Where there are dissimilar products or services, to add up all the costs and allocate them evenly to each item or each hour worked would be unfair: units of low worth would be allocated the same amount of costs as units of high worth. There are fairer ways of sharing costs but they require a little more effort. First, it is necessary to distinguish between direct and indirect costs:

- **Direct costs** are those which can be traced to a particular unit, such as the cost of wood to make a chair or the wages paid to make it.
- **Indirect costs** are those costs which cannot be traced to a particular unit, for example the use of a telephone, insurance and transport.

It will be easy to allocate direct costs as they relate to specific units. The indirect costs must be shared out fairly in some way. One way is to base the spread on direct costs.

An example

The costs for a clothes manufacturer are estimated to be:

Material	Dress A 100 @ £6.00 ea =	£600
	Dress B 200 @ £4.50 ea =	£900
Wages	Dress A 100 @ £4.00 ea =	£400
	Dress B 200 @ £3.00 ea =	£600

The indirect costs such as telephone, delivery and stationery are expected to be £2,000.

| | Total direct costs | |
	Dress A	Dress B
Material	£600	£900
Wages	£400	£600
	£1,000	£1,500

Total direct costs are therefore £2,500 (1,000 for dress A plus £1,500 for dress B). This means that for every £1 we spend on direct costs we spend £0.80 (£2,000 ÷ £2,500) on indirect costs.

Therefore it could be said that the indirect costs incurred by dress A are $1,000 \times 0.80 = £800$ and by dress B $1,500 \times 0.80 = £1,200$.

	£800		£1,200
Total costs	£1,800		£2,700
Price per unit:			
1,800 ÷ 100	£18.00		
2,700 ÷ 200			£13.50

The calculations could also have been based on materials or wages rather than total direct costs. Choose the most relevant option or, alternatively, where there is little difference between the costs of the products, select the easiest.

The indirect costs of a home-based business are likely to be relatively low and therefore not particularly significant. Where this is the case, do not spend a lot of time deciding how to allocate them to individual units. A simple calculation will suffice.

Remember, the calculations are only as accurate as the assumptions and estimates made. The prices should be used as a yardstick when considering other factors such as your competitors' prices.

How low can sales prices be set?

To make a profit, sales need to be greater than costs. In our previous examples we have considered costs to be total costs. In certain circumstances, by splitting costs into fixed and variable costs it is possible to undercut the total cost price but still improve the firm's financial position.

Fixed costs are those costs that stay constant, in the long term, whether business activity increases or decreases. They are very often the same as indirect costs.

Variable costs are those costs that vary with business activity and are often synonymous with direct costs.

Undercutting

A rug-making business has the following estimated annual costs:

Fixed costs (stationery, telephone, etc)	£1,000 total
Variable costs (labour and raw materials)	£62 per rug

Table 7.4 shows the profit or loss for various selling prices based on the sale of 100 units.

Table 7.4   Profit and loss results on the sale of 100 units

Selling Price £	Profit/(Loss) £
58	(1,400)
60	(1,200)
62	(1,000)
65	(700)
72	0
75	300

No profit is made until the selling price generates sales that exceed total costs, that is once the selling price is more than £72.

If the selling price is below £62 sales will not even pay for the raw materials and labour. In this instance it would not usually be viable to continue trading. Once a selling price of over £62 is achieved, losses are reduced and the situation is improved. It is better to sell 100 items at £63 and make a loss of £900 than to sell none and still have to pay fixed costs of £1,000. This is because any amount over £62 can be used to pay for some of the fixed costs. (When a business is frequently unable to meet its fixed costs, closure should be considered.)

It can be particularly useful to price in this way for a large order if you have the spare capacity and have already covered the fixed costs with other orders. In this situation any amount above the variable costs will be profit. Such a price may well be lower than that of competitors trying to recover their fixed costs, but it is important to consider the effect of such a pricing policy on your other customers and the potential problems of setting a precedent for lower prices.

You must consider all the factors determining price, not just the financial calculations.

8 *Getting paid*

How can debt collection be improved?

Cash is the lifeblood of any business. Too little will, at best, restrict your business operations; at worst it may result in bankruptcy or liquidation. It therefore makes sense to collect promptly all monies due to the business.

There are three important aspects to getting paid promptly. They are:

- ensure all sales documents, goods and services are satisfactory;
- understand your customers' payment systems;
- chase payment.

Ensure that all sales documents, goods and services are satisfactory

Customers will only pay for goods and services with which they are wholly satisfied. Take great care to ensure that this is the case. Rectifying errors will result in delayed payment and will use up some of your valuable time.

Make sure that all customers are aware of your terms and conditions of sale and agree to follow them. These are likely to include such matters as return of goods and credit period allowed. Terms and conditions of sale are often printed on the reverse side of the sales invoice.

Check the details of the invoice to be certain that you have neither under- nor overcharged your customer. Any errors will undermine the customer's confidence in your abilities but only overcharging will be brought to your attention.

Understand your customers' payment systems

A little time spent understanding how and when your customers pay you can reap benefits. If you are dealing with the public, you are unlikely to be allowing large amounts of credit. However, collecting money on or shortly after pay day may prove more fruitful than at other times.

When dealing with trade customers you will find it invaluable to learn about their payment system. This knowledge can then be used to optimise your chances of prompt payment. Three tips here are:

● Find out what information and documents are required before an invoice is accepted and processed. Arrange matters so that you comply with these requirements every time.
● Find out who deals with your account so that you can quickly discuss any problems with the appropriate person.
● Many businesses pay suppliers periodically – often at the end of each month. To do this they will generally close the ledger on or near the end of the month. Any invoices received before this point will be processed and included for payment. Invoices received afterwards will be processed and paid the following month. Thus, an invoice presented a day late could result in payment being delayed by one month.

Chasing payment

It is important to chase payment from customers, as many businesses and individuals will place non-chasing creditors at the bottom of their payment pile. However, it is vital to remain reasonable in your demands, as good customer relationships are important for future sales.

Before chasing payment for any debt that has become overdue, make certain that the customer is aware of your credit terms and that there are no queries on the transaction. To chase in these circumstances could irritate the customer.

There are three main ways of chasing your customers for payment – by telephone, letter or in person. The telephone is probably the most convenient method to use, particularly in the early stages. It is informal, quick, direct and gives immediate feedback. A personal visit will probably be as effective as a telephone call but may be perceived as being more intimidatory unless this is the norm for your business (for example, if you are a window cleaner).

Customers usually consider a letter to be a more formal approach. It is, therefore, best used when you feel other approaches are no longer proving fruitful.

I recommend that you send a sequence of three letters. Examples illustrating the composition of three letters of increasing strength are given on pages 80–82 in Figure 8.1, 8.2 and 8.3 respectively. Each letter should be on headed paper, give all the relevant details (such as invoice and account numbers and amount due) and set a time limit for a response.

All letters should be polite but firm. In the later letters it may be appropriate to explain that no further orders will be accepted and that further action will be taken if necessary. Keep a copy of each letter and send them by recorded delivery.

Other tips for improving debt collection:

1. Keep the pressure up.
2. Try speaking to someone other than your usual contact, such as the owner, the accountant or the managing director.
3. Consider using a debt collection agency.
4. Consider charging interest on any overdue debts. Although some customers will be prompted to pay on time considering the following:
   – Under the Late Payment of Commercial Debts (Interest) Act 1998, a business has a legal right to claim interest, if it wishes, when another business is late paying its bills. From 1

Mr J Brown
The Managing Director
ABC & Co Ltd
Unit 3
Brooke End Industrial Estate
Staffs XY10 2LY

The VG Typing Bureau
10 Church Road
Brooke End
Staffs XY10 1ZA

Our Ref LG/731/123/01

Your Ref 4Q2/YT

19/10/01

Dear Mr Brown

RE: Non-payment of account number 731

I would like to bring the above item to your attention. The amount of £531.21 relating to our invoice number 123 (a copy of which is enclosed) is now 30 days overdue.

Would you please ensure payment within the next seven days.

Yours sincerely

Linda Groves

If payment has already been made please disregard this correspondence.

Figure 8.1   Letter requesting payment

VGT
Proprietor B J Black

Mr J Brown
The Managing Director
ABC & Co Ltd
Unit 3
Brooke End Industrial Estate
Staffs XY10 2LY

The VG Typing Bureau
10 Church Road
Brooke End
Staffs XY10 1ZA

Our Ref LG/731/123/02

Your Ref 4Q2/YT

26/10/01

Dear Mr Brown

With reference to our letter LG/731/123/01 dated 19/10/01 the amount £531.21 on account number 731 is now significantly overdue. If this amount is not forthcoming within the next seven days we will be unable to provide you with any further services.

Yours sincerely

Linda Grove

Figure 8.2   Further letter requesting payment

Mr J Brown
The Managing Director
ABC & Co Ltd
Unit 3
Brooke End Industrial Estate
Staffs XY10 2LY

The VG Typing Bureau
10 Church Road
Brooke End
Staffs XY10 1ZA

Our Ref LG/731/123/03

Your Ref 4Q2/YT

2/11/01

Dear Mr Brown

With reference to our letter LG/731/123/02 if the amount of £531.21 is not received within seven days we shall refer this matter to our solicitor.

Yours sincerely

Linda Grove

Figure 8.3   Letter requesting payment and threatening legal action

November 2002 this will be available to all businesses and the public sector, but until then it is available to all small businesses (of fewer than 50 employees) on contracts agreed after 1 November 2000.

- It may deter some customers.
- Customers may see it as permission to pay later.
- Customers may pay late but refuse to pay the interest; although you may be entitled to it, chasing it may not be cost-effective.

5. Some factoring companies offer a service whereby they buy your debts for cash and then collect them. They will not advance the whole amount but will pay the balance on collection of the debt.

Factoring companies offer a variety of other services but may be unwilling to deal with very small businesses. To find out more you can contact the Factors and Discounters Association or visit www. payontime.co.uk (address is given on page 44).

How can the risk of bad debts be reduced?

Bad debts are amounts due from customers that are unlikely ever to be paid. One large, bad debt could be sufficient to ruin a home-based business. At the very least, bad debts reduce profits and worsen cash flow and can be a waste of your time and effort. There are a number of steps you can take to reduce your exposure to bad debts:

1. The larger the bad debt, the greater the effect will be on the business, so take care when allowing high levels of credit.
2. If you consider that a customer is unlikely to pay, act immediately and cease to trade with him or her.
3. Obtain credit references for the level of credit you propose to allow the customer and do not exceed this limit. However, credit references are no guarantee of payment. They quickly become

out of date and are often, unavoidably, based on out-of-date information.

4. If practical, reduce the credit period you allow. This may not be feasible if your competitors are offering generous credit terms and competition is strong.

5. Insist on cash on delivery or cash with order. Even a cash on delivery policy has its risks from forged banknotes or stolen cheques, credit cards or building society cheques. To reduce the risk from loss due to fraudulent payment it is important to be very careful when accepting payment by any of these methods.
    - **Cash**. Be particularly careful if you aware of forgeries circulating in your area. Consider purchasing an ultraviolet machine which can quickly detect forged bank notes.
    - **Cheques**. When accepting payment by cheque insist on a cheque guarantee card. If you follow stipulated bank procedure correctly when accepting payment, the bank will honour the cheque. A cheque card does not guarantee a cheque that exceeds its limit, which is usually set at £50 or £100.

      A cheque without an appropriate guarantee can bounce. If in doubt, ask for further identification such as a driver's licence, passport or a current bill with home address on it so that the customer can be traced. Alternatively, wait until the cheque has been cleared at the bank before providing goods or services.
    - **Credit cards**. If you follow the procedure laid down by the credit card companies, they are likely to honour all transactions. You will, on the other hand, have to pay a percentage of each credit card transaction to the card company.
    - **Building society cheques**. These are generally regarded to be as good as cash. Unfortunately, this may not be the case. A sensible precaution would be to ask for indentification or wait until the cheque has cleared.

6. Listen to other traders who identify who they consider to be a bad risk. A customer may start using your business because he or she has been refused credit elsewhere.

7. Obtain credit insurance. This will offer protection against customers who do not pay. It can be difficult to obtain this type of insurance but it is particularly useful if your business relies on the custom of a handful of clients. Don't forget to speak to your bank if you need advice.

How do I deal with disputes?

Disputes can be time consuming, costly and damaging. Try to resolve them politely and quickly. Before incurring any additional expense, consider carefully. The cost of further action may be more than the disputed transaction. If you attempt to resolve a dispute informally consider the following:

● Keeping calm and being polite and sympathetic may help to pacify the customer.
● Are your goods or services wholly or partly at fault?
● If you have any doubts ask a third party for an opinion.
● Can a compromise be reached that satisfies both parties?
● Has the customer incurred any additional expense?
● Is your reputation at risk?
● Is the dispute with a valued customer?
● Are your records and documents correct and up to date? If they are, use them in your communications with the customer to help make your point.

Keep a comprehensive record of the dispute. This will be invaluable if it cannot be amicably resolved and you decide to take further action. Once you have decided that further action is called for there is a number of options open to you. Consider using the services of an arbitrator. You can contact the Chartered Institute of Arbitrators on 020 7404 4023 at:

Chartered Institute of Arbitrators
12 Bloomsbury Square
London WC1A 2LP

It may be appropriate to use the county court, where your case will be heard with minimal formalities. Your local county court will supply you with more details. A third option is to consult a solicitor.

What action can be taken if a debtor will not pay?

Once you have ascertained that a customer will not pay, any further action on your part will cost money. Be sure the action is worth it or you may find that the only beneficiaries are the lawyers.

As with disputes, bad debts can be pursued in the county court. If necessary, consult a solicitor.

9 *Planning and control*

What is planning and control?

Planning is all about looking ahead. It therefore involves estimates and assumptions about the future. Planning will help to formulate expected future performance.

As the business develops it is important that actual performance is monitored against that predicted. This will help the management or controller of the business to identify problems early and thus take steps to solve them.

The main element for implementing a planning and control system for a business is the preparation and monitoring of budgets.

Why is planning and control necessary?

Planning can provide a lot of useful information, including:

- how much to borrow;
- how much to order;
- staff levels required;
- which equipment to buy;
- expected profits.

Planning can be central to your work in the early days of the business as there will be no historical data on which to base decisions. It will also help to determine whether the business is likely to be a viable proposition. Careful control will quickly identify any potential problems, such as slow payment by debtors or insufficient stock. These can then be promptly rectified or accommodated.

What is a budget?

A budget is a quantitative plan. The most common budget is thought to be the cash budget, otherwise known as the cash flow forecast. The cash flow forecast sets out the expected cash and cheque receipts and the payments to enable expected finance requirements to be estimated.

There are no mandatory formats for budgets. Choose one to suit you and your business needs. If the budgets are to be used to raise finance, they should be clear and legible and, if necessary, in the format prescribed by the proposed lender. Budgets should be prepared to meet your firm's requirements. Often budgets are prepared on a monthly basis.

Which budgets should be prepared?

Most businesses run from home are likely to find a cash flow forecast and a budgeted profit and loss account both essential and sufficient. Other possibilities include:

- sales budget;
- purchase budget;
- forecast balance sheet;
- production budget.

However, because of the likely size of the home-based operation and close control by the owner, few formal budgets will be necessary.

How is a budget prepared?

For an owner-controlled business, operated from home, there are two main aspects to preparing budgets:

- estimating and making assumptions;
- collating and calculating.

If the budgets are to be used in the business by someone other than the owner, a salesman for example, it will also be necessary to consider any behavioural aspects of the budget, in other words the psychological effects of a budget on you and your staff.

Estimating and making assumptions

Budgets are all about planning for the future so, of necessity, they include many estimates and assumptions. Virtually all home-based businesses will be in the position of needing to assess income and expenditure. The necessary assumptions will vary from firm to firm but may include:

- credit taken by customers;
- timing of other receipts;
- credit allowed by suppliers;
- timing of other payments;
- level of pay increases;
- availability of labour;
- availability of raw materials.

When estimating sales use the following as a guide:

- past trends;
- marketplace trends;
- orders;

- reports from the sales force;
- market research information;
- results of other similar businesses;
- any statements made by customers.

When estimating payments use the following as a guide:

- past trends;
- any statements from suppliers about future price increases;
- any other information available from suppliers (cost of telephone calls per minute, and so forth);
- marketplace trends;
- costs of similar businesses;
- results from any trials, for example making sample jewellery to establish the cost of raw materials and labour;
- information from government departments which will explain when VAT, National Insurance, PAYE and taxation are payable.

Estimates can often be easier to make if they are broken down into their various constituents and evaluated on a daily basis.

Estimating sales

Consider a home-based business selling children's toys on a party plan basis.

Average expected attendance at each party plan	8 people
On average 75 per cent make a purchase	6 people
Average spend per person	£10
Therefore total spend per party	£60

The expected number of party plans in the year is shown in Table 9.1.

Table 9.1   Expected number of party plans

	No of parties	
	Per week	Total
12 weeks	0	(holidays, sickness, etc)
30 weeks	2	60
10 weeks	3	30
Total number of parties in the year		90

Therefore annual sales are projected to be £5,400 (60 × 90).

Estimating telephone costs

British Telecom and other providers of telephone services will readily supply details of rental and call costs. All you need to do then is estimate the number of calls you expect to make (see Table 9.2).

Table 9.2   Estimated number of business calls

Estimated number of calls per day	6
Consisting of:	
Local calls	3
Long distance calls	3
Estimated duration of a call	5 minutes
The call rates are local calls	30p per minute
Long distance calls	50p per minute

The cost per day of business is estimated to be:

Local calls (3 × 5 × 0.3)	£4.50
Long distance	£7.50
Total costs per day	£12.00

The business, it is anticipated, will make phone calls five days per week for 48 weeks of the year. Therefore, the annual cost will be 12 × 48 × 5 = £2,880.

Accurate assumptions and estimate are very difficult to achieve. It can, therefore, be useful to prepare a number of budgets using different assumptions and estimates. If you have access to a computer spreadsheet facility it is fairly easy to prepare a number of budgets based on a variety of information. Once the spreadsheet is set up the software does most of the work for you should you need calculations based on new figures.

Preparing budgets by hand can be extremely time consuming. To save time, consider preparing your budgets on the basis of the following:

- optimistic expectations;
- pessimistic expectations;
- most likely expectations.

If your home-based firm has been operating on a static basis and is expected to continue to do so, only one budget, based on the most likely expectations, may be necessary.

Always include a small contingency in your budgets. If you have an overdraft facility part of it will remain unused; but if you have to borrow more it does not present your planning skills in a very good light.

Don't forget that the budget you prepare will be only as accurate as the assumptions and estimates you have used in preparing it.

Collating and calculating

Once you have made your estimates and assumptions it is time to collect them all together and prepare your budget.

Budgeted profit and loss account statements and budget balance sheets are prepared in the same way as their historical versions (see pages 125–31) except that expected, rather than actual, results are used.

The layout of other budgets will vary. They will often be set out so

	Jan	Feb	Mar	April	May	June	July	Aug	Sept	Oct	Nov	Dec	Total
Receipts													
Sales		300	300	350	350	400	400	400	450	450	500	500	4,400
Loan	1,000												1,000
Other													
Total	1,000	300	300	350	350	400	400	400	450	450	500	500	5,400
Payments													
Materials	250	200	150	150	150	200	200	200	250	250	250	250	2,500
Outworkers	10	10	10	10	10	30	30	30	50	50	50	50	340
Equipment	300												300
Advertising	100	20	20	20	20	20	20	20	20	20	20	20	320
Other overheads	100	100	100	100	100	100	100	100	100	100	100	100	1,200
Total	760	330	280	280	280	350	350	350	420	420	420	420	4,660
Opening bank balance	0	240	210	230	300	370	420	470	520	550	580	660	0
Closing bank balance	240	210	230	300	370	420	470	520	550	580	660	740	740

Table 9.3 A cash flow statement

as to show both monthly and total amounts for each category in the budget. Choose a format to suit you and your business. If you are preparing a cash flow statement to help raise finance, check with the potential lender to establish whether there are any particular formats they wish to use.

One of the most important budgets you will prepare will be the cash flow statement. Planning and control of cash flow is essential. A lack of cash can lead to a curtailing of operations or, at worst, to liquidation or bankruptcy. If surplus funds are available it is advantageous to invest them to generate additional income. However, you must ensure that funds are available for use in the business when required.

When collating the cash budget, bear in mind that both the amount and the timing of the cash flows are significant. For example, credit customers will pay after the sale has been made, so it is necessary to enter sales cash and cheques in the month that you expect to receive them rather than in the month when the sale takes place.

Be meticulous in recording all your forecast payments and receipts. After all, the bank will not be very impressed if you prepare a cash flow statement that does not provide for the payment of bank interest, charges and capital loan repayments when they are due. Where categories of receipts or payments are immaterial they can be totalled and shown as one. Possible receipts include:

● sales income;
● loans;
● capital introduced;
● refunds and rebates.

Possible payments include:

● materials
● labour costs;
● equipment and machinery;
● motor vehicles;
● advertising and marketing;

- heating and light;
- postage and telephone;
- PAYE;
- National Insurance;
- taxation;
- VAT;
- transport costs;
- packaging;
- stationery;
- insurance;
- training;
- professional expenses (for example, solicitors' and accountants' fees);
- bank interest;
- capital loan repayments;
- other interest payments;
- personal salary and drawings.

An example of a simple cash flow statement is given in Table 9.3 (page 93).

Behavioural aspects of budgeting

A home-based entrepreneur may look to budgets as a useful way to set targets for his employees: such objectives can indeed motivate staff. Nevertheless, the budgets need to be not only testing but achievable. If goals are seen as being unattainable staff are unlikely to attempt to meet them. Conversely, if targets are easily attained staff may sit back and thus miss some lucrative opportunities.

10 *Keeping basic books and records*

Is keeping records necessary?

I know that this is bad news to many of you, but keeping books and records is essential. When running your own business you will need to know the answer to many questions:

- How many pictures have I sold?
- How much does each picture cost to make?
- What profit have I made?
- How much does Mr Smith owe me?
- How much do I owe Mr Jones?

Without proper records you will not be able to answer these questions accurately. Your books and records must also satisfy the requirements of the Inland Revenue and where VAT is involved, Customs and Excise, otherwise you could find yourself paying a substantial fine.

Do I need to employ an accountant?

The good news is that you don't have to. There is no legal requirement to employ an accountant to keep your books and records. If you are a limited company you may need to employ an auditor. My advice is to do the bookkeeping yourself if possible. This will save money and ensure that you are up to date with what is happening in your business.

Is it necessary to open a business bank account?

No, it is not essential but it can be quite useful. A separate bank account will help to keep personal and business transactions separate and so should simplify bookkeeping and accounts preparation. Unfortunately, charges for business bank accounts are often higher than for a personal account, but many banks will offer lower rates for the first few years.

Be very careful to keep accurate books and records if you decide to operate without a business bank account.

Should I keep computerised records?

Only if you want to. There is no specific requirement by the Inland Revenue or Customs and Excise for records to be computerised or manual. Either is acceptable, so the choice is yours. A computer can be particularly useful where the number of accounting transactions is high or where a proprietor can use the computer for functions other than bookkeeping, possibly budgeting and stock control. Frequently, a new home-based business will be small enough for the records to be kept manually.

If you do decide to have computerised records, choose wisely. If you propose to maintain the records yourself, assess the computer and its software so as to be sure that you buy a suitable package. In cases where an accountant, bookkeeper or similar person is to keep your records, satisfy yourself that he or she is adequately experienced and knowledgeable.

How often should I update my books?

It is very important that you keep your books and records up to date so that you will always know your businesses's position. By being disciplined and writing up your books regularly and frequently, this will never become onerous. If you have only a few transactions you might find a monthly update is sufficient. On the other hand, a business with many transactions may require the books to be updated daily.

What books and records should I keep?

As a minimum most businesses will require:

- sales invoices;
- purchase invoices;
- cash book.

What is a sales invoice?

A sales invoice is a document, issued to customers, showing information about the goods or services you are supplying. If you are registered for VAT you will be required to produce tax invoices. A typical tax invoice is shown in Figure 10.1 on page 99. Even if you are not required to prepare tax invoices, you may still find it appropriate to provide similar information. Obviously, some of the information such as VAT number, VAT rate and the amount of VAT is not relevant and can be omitted.

Quantity	Description and Price	£
	From: A Smith Jones Street Leicester	Sales Invoice No 123 Date & Tax point 30/07/01 VAT registered No 1234
	To: B. White Black Street Derby	
3	Pottery Bowls @ £40.00 each	120.00
	Total (exclusive of VAT)	120.00
	VAT @ 17½ %	21.00
	Total	141.00
	To be paid within 30 days of invoice tax point	

Figure 10.1 Sales invoice

When you produce a sales invoice, you should also make a copy for your own records and as evidence of the transaction for the Inland Revenue and Customs and Excise. A carbon copy is acceptable but a photocopy will not be well received. If, for some reason, you have to cancel a sales invoice before issuing it, keep it with the copy so that, if ever challenged by Inland Revenue or Customs and Excise, you can prove the invoice was not issued.

What is a purchase invoice?

A purchase invoice is a document issued to you by your suppliers, showing information about the goods or services you have purchased (they are your suppliers' sales invoices).

Your purchase invoices should be kept to confirm to the Inland Revenue and Customs and Excise the business purchases you have made.

What is a cash book for?

The cash book is a record for all the receipts and payments made by your business whether by cheque or cash. For security and convenience many businesses deal mainly in cheques, but the nature of your business may dictate whether you use cash, cheques or both.

The cash book needs to contain sufficient information for you to determine:

- when you received money;
- how much you received;
- who paid you;
- how they paid and for what;
- when you made payments;
- how much you paid;
- who you paid;
- how you paid and for what.

A possible layout for a cash book page is set out in Tables 10.1 and 10.2. The layout can be adapted to suit the needs of the business. For instance, where a business has cash and bank transactions the total column can be divided into two, one column for cheques and the other for cash.

What should I write in the cash book?

Receipts

The following sample transactions have been entered on Table 10.1 to illustrate how the cash book works.

A) 01/04/01 cash sale made to Q White on sales invoice number 125. White paid by cheque.

	Amounts
VAT	£17.50
NET	£100.00
TOTAL	£117.50

B 06/04/01 money received from P Black relating to sales invoice number 120. This was a credit sale.

	Amounts
VAT	£98.00
NET	£560.00
TOTAL	£658.00

C) 12/04/01 the business receives some dividends from shares it owns. The amount is £51.25. The divided counterfoil is the tenth in the dividend file.

D) 30/04/01 the business is expanding so you put some of your savings – £5,000.00 – into it.

Table 10.1   Cash book: receipts

	Date	Details	Ref	Total	VAT sales	Credit sales	Cash sales	Capital	Sundry
	(1)	(2)	£ (3)	£ (4)	£ (5)	£ (6)	£ (6)	£ (7)	(8)
A	01/04/01	Q White	125	117.50	17.50		100.00		
B	06/04/01	P Black	120	658.00	98.00	560.00			
C	1204/01	TAB Industries	Div File 10	51.25					51.25 Dividends
D	30/04/01	T Owner	Cap File 1	5,000.00				5,000.00	
E	30/04/01	Totals		5,826.75	115.50	560.00	100.00	5,000.00	51.25

(1) Entering the date ensures that you know exactly when a transaction was conducted so that you can establish your bank balance at any point in time. It will also help in tracing transactions.

(2) Enter here sufficient information to enable you to identify who had paid you and for what. When completing this column it is better to enter too much information rather than too little. Do not rely on your memory, which may prove unreliable, particularly once transactions are a few months old.

(3) A reference column can be very useful if used properly. The idea is to give every entry a reference number so that the document explaining the transaction can be found easily; for example money received, relating to a sale, would be referenced to the relevant sales invoice by its number.

(4) This column identifies the total of the money paid into the bank.

Columns (5) to (9) categorise the money you receive according to the nature of the transaction. This will help you or your accountant to prepare the year -end accounts. These headings are flexible and should be selected to meet your business information needs.

(5) VAT charged on your sales does not belong to you or your business and must be paid to Customs and Excise. It must, therefore, be clearly identified in your books and records. Obviously, if you are not registered for VAT, there is no requirement to maintain a VAT column.

(6) Credit sales are those sales where the customer has the goods or service before paying. Cash sales are those sales where the customer has the goods or service at the same time as paying. It can be useful to keep them separate to aid identifying which customers have paid.

(7) Capital refers to any money that you introduce to the business.

(8) It is always useful to keep a 'sundry' column to record any non-typical transactions. Leave plenty of space for this column so that you can clearly describe these unusual transactions.

E) Usually at the end of the month, the cash book is added up and the totals checked. Note that the totals of columns (5) to (9) inclusive, should add up to the total of column (4). This is a useful check on your addition.

Payments

The following sample transactions have been entered on Figure 10.3 to illustrate how the cash book works for payments.

A) 05/04/01 payment to P James for materials supplied on invoice number 70.

	Amounts
VAT	£35.00
NET	£200.00
TOTAL	£235.00

B) 10/04/01 payment to Book & Co for car repairs on invoice number 74.

	Amounts
VAT	£61.25
NET	£350.00
TOTAL	£411.25

C) 20/04/01 payment of April salary to Mr Read £575.00.

D) 30/04/01 payment of April PAYE and NIC to the Inland Revenue £230.00.

E) 30/04/01 bank charges deducted from your account.

Table 10.2 Cash book: payments

	Date	Details	Ref	Cheque No (1)	Total £	VAT £	Materials (2)	Motor Expenses £ (2)	Wages £ (2)	PAYE & NIC (2)	Drawings (2)	Sundry (2)
A	05/04/01	P James	70	005730	235.00	35.00	200.00					
B	10/04/01	Book & Co Car Repairs	74	005731	411.25	61.25		350.00				
C	20/04/01	Mr Read	April salary	005732	575.00				575.00			
D	30/04/01	Inland Revenue	April PAYE & NIC	005733	230.00					230.00		
E	30/04/01	Bank charges	Bank file 12		35.25	5.25						Bank charges 30.00
	30/04/01	Totals			1,486.50	101.50	200.00	350.00	575.00	230.00		30.00

(1) If you keep a record of cheque numbers you will find it a lot easier to check your cash book details with the bank. It will also help matters if a cheque is lost or has to be cancelled.

(2) Keep a record of payments made according to the type of goods or services purchased – this will vary from business to business – so that you know where you are spending your money. This is useful information for you in conducting your business and is necessary for your end of year accounts. The Inland Revenue will provide you will a leaflet outlining the information they require.

(3) Drawings is a record of monies taken by the owner(s) for private use.

	Amounts
VAT	£5.25
NET	£30.00
TOTAL	£35.25

How do I work out my bank balance?

At the end of each month it is worth working out the amount you have in your bank account. This can be done as follows:

(a) If you have cash in hand at the bank

	£
Amount in the bank at the start of the month	500
Add the amount received in the month	1,250
Subtract the amount paid out in the month	900
Equals the amount in the bank at the end of the month	850

(b) If you are overdrawn at the bank

	£
Amount in the bank at the start of the month	150 od
Increase the overdraft by the amount paid out in that month	700
Decrease the overdraft by the amount received in that month	770
Equals the amount in the bank at the end of the month	80 od

How will I know how much money my business is owed?

People who owe your business money are known as debtors. A simple way to control this side of your business is to keep all your unpaid invoices together. When you receive payment mark the invoice as paid and file it with other paid invoices. Referring to your unpaid invoice file will tell you how much your customers owe you. This system should work well if your volume of unpaid invoices is small. If this system would result in a large pile of unpaid invoices, you will need to consider the more sophisticated system described in Chapter 11.

How will I know how much I owe to my suppliers?

Use the same system as described above but apply it to your purchase invoices. People your business owes money to are known as creditors.

How will I know that I have invoiced all my customers?

It is very important to keep track of this because, if you do not invoice your customers, it is extremely unlikely that you will get paid. The most important thing is to make a record of the sale or job done as soon as possible. This could be achieved by producing the sales invoice at the moment of sale. Where this is not convenient, keep an intermediate record, such as a notebook, which you carry with you at all times. This can later be used to prepare the sales invoice. If the latter method is used, cancel the entries in the notebook as the sales invoice is produced and make a note of the invoice number against the cancelled note. This should prevent you from invoicing customers twice.

How do I make sure that I pay only for items that I receive?

Make a record of everything you receive when you receive it – again a notebook would be useful. Do not sign for anything unless you have thoroughly checked it first. If it is not practical to check the delivery immediately, then make a note, near your signature, indicating that the goods have not been checked. When you receive a supplier's invoice check it against your delivery records before paying it. Cancel your delivery record and make a note of the cheque and invoice numbers against the cancelled note. This will also help you to avoid paying twice for goods and services supplied.

Will wages records be required?

Only if you have employees. Directors of a limited company are classed as employees but sole traders and partners are not. Monies taken by sole traders or partners are known as drawings and should be recorded in the cash book.

If your business has one or more employees the Inland Revenue will supply the necessary documents to be completed, together with explanatory booklets, or you can buy a suitable computer package.

What other books and records will I need?

The essential books and records have already been described above and these should be quite adequate for most small home-based businesses.

If you feel that these are not sufficient for your business, more detailed books and records are identified in the next chapter.

The best guide to the books and records you should keep is your business – keep books and records to provide you with the information you need to run it efficiently.

11 *Keeping track of purchases, sales, debtors, creditors and stock*

The minimum level of records has already been outlined in Chapter 10. This will be perfectly adequate for many home-based operations, but some will require more detail because of the size and nature of the business.

Which businesses need detailed records?

Ask yourself the following questions:

- How much do customers owe?
- How much are suppliers owed?
- How much stock is there?
- How much did the stock cost?
- Which orders are pending?

If you obtain quick, satisfactory answers from the basic books and records, you are maintaining adequate records and need proceed no further. If you do not, you must consider using some or all of the records covered in this chapter.

Why is it important to monitor sales?

Sales generate profit for a business. Often home-based businesses put a lot of hard work into developing sales, so do not waste time and profit by forgetting orders or failing to invoice accurately.

How can sales be monitored?

There are four main areas to consider:

- sales orders;
- delivery;
- time records;
- sales invoice preparation.

How can orders be controlled?

For some firms an order will result in an immediate sale, while for others there may be a significant time lag. The longer the time between order and sale the greater the likelihood of the order being lost, forgotten or incorrectly fulfilled, and therefore the greater the need for control.

To avoid errors, orders are best recorded in writing when received. Send a copy to the customer for confirmation of the details. Sequentially pre-numbered order forms are useful, as any missing orders can quickly be identified.

Once an order has been completed and invoiced, mark it as

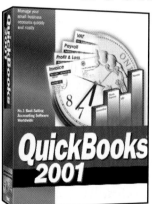

QuickBooks

Although starting your own business is exciting and challenging it can also provide major headaches. Keeping on top of who owes you what and when as well as what you owe is fundamental to business success – especially considering that businesses can fold these days owing as little as £1,500.

Setting up in business means getting to grips with such issues as budgeting, invoicing, profit and loss forecasting, supplier management, payroll as well as managing obligations such as tax and VAT.

But help is at hand. Investing in accounting software such as *QuickBooks* – designed specifically for the SME – is a cost-effective way to put all this important information at your fingertips, ensuring you've more time to spend growing your business.

For many businesses, time is a critical feature. With many business managers working a 12-14 hour day, the provision of readily available information on their business tends to be something they think about at the end of the day. As the business grows, how does the owner manager manage with demands of staffing, payroll, suppliers, and look after his customers at the same time?

For Andrew Blackburn, the solution lay in choosing a software package that met his needs. In March 1997 he set up the Extreme Pizza Company originally as a take-away employing five part time staff. The business has now expanded to two full-time and eight part-time staff.

'Running a small business is a constant juggling act', says Andrew. 'Apart from cooking and hosting the restaurant, I'm also keeping track of orders, stock and overall management. I therefore have very little time to spend on accounts, so I need a software package that is quick, efficient and easy to use'.

Andrew now needs to spend only 30 minutes a day updating his books. He uses *QuickBooks* to log invoices from food and drink and packaging suppliers and to produce instant reports on the best selling products and overall sales analysis.

'Now more of my time and energy is focused on growing my business – not wading through complex and manual accounts'. Recognising the pressures of running a business, many successful managers today are choosing to invest in systems such as *QuickBooks* to free up their time and give them a competitive edge.

completed and enter the sales invoice number. This should ensure that uncompleted and un-invoiced orders can be identified and processed easily.

How can deliveries be controlled?

Many disputes arise because somehow the goods despatched are not the same as the goods that arrive. To help avoid disagreements, issue all deliveries with a document recording the quantity and type of goods being sent. Ask your customers to sign the document to confirm the items received. This document is known as a despatch or delivery note and should be kept as evidence of goods received by the customer.

If you do not deliver the goods personally ask the delivery service to obtain the signature and return the delivery document or provide other similar evidence of receipt of goods.

Time records

Home-based businesses providing services will not require delivery documents. They provide expertise, not goods. To keep track of work in hand, it may be beneficial to maintain some form of time record.

Often, services are charged at an hourly rate. To charge a client correctly it is, therefore, essential to know how much time has been spent on each job.

Where there are a few staff and only a handful of different jobs at any one time, a simple diary record should be sufficient. Alternatively, more detailed tabular time sheets would facilitate collating total hours worked per job.

Maintaining accurate sales invoice preparation

The sales invoice is the document that informs the customer of the goods or service you have supplied, how much you require for this and when you expect to be paid by. Customers do not like to be over-charged or asked to pay for items and service they have not received. It creates extra administrative work for all concerned and may lower their confidence in your business abilities. Unidentified undercharging will result in a loss of profit.

When preparing the invoice, check the details of any documents that back up the sales invoice such as:

- price lists;
- sales order;
- delivery document;
- time sheets.

Check all calculations to ensure that they are correct. If mistakes arise, your customers are likely to ask you to send a credit note to rectify any differences. The credit note will be used by the customer to reduce the amount owed to your business. An example of a credit note is shown in Figure 11.1. To avoid any confusion, make sure that credit notes are clearly distinguishable from sales invoices. They could, for example, be a different colour.

Why is it important to monitor purchases?

Purchases reduce the amount of profit that a business makes. It is, therefore, important that they are carefully controlled. This should ensure that only those items required are ordered and paid for.

There are many errors that may arise:

| From: | A Smith | Credit Note No 3 |
| To: | B. White | |

From:	A Smith Jones Street Leicester	Credit Note No 3 Date & Tax point 05/04/01 VAT registered No 1234
To:	B. White Black Street Derby	

Quantity	Description and Price	£
1	Cracked Pottery Bowl @ £40.00 each	40.00
	Total (exclusive of VAT)	40.00
	VAT @ 17½ %	7.00
	Total	47.00

Figure 11.1 Credit note

- incorrectly priced invoices;
- arithmetically incorrect invoices;
- unsolicited goods;
- faulty goods;
- incorrect quantities.

If purchases are not monitored you could end up paying for someone else's mistakes.

How can purchasing errors be avoided?

To ensure that you pay the correct amount for the goods you order and receive, it is important to keep a record of the prices agreed with the supplier, the goods you order and the goods you receive.

A useful way of recording the prices and the goods ordered is to prepare a purchase order. A copy of this can be sent to the supplier who will then have a record of your requirements.

When the goods are received, record the fact, prepare a 'goods inwards' note, and check the details against your purchase order. If there are any discrepancies notify the supplier immediately.

When you receive invoices, check them against the relevant purchase orders and goods inwards notes before processing them for payment.

How can more detailed debtor information be maintained?

It is important to know how much each customer owes at any point in time and to what these amounts relate. This will facilitate credit control and resolving disputes. It can be done by keeping a separate record for each customer, often called a 'sales ledger account', which will record together all transactions for a particular customer. Transactions will include:

- sales invoices;
- receipts;
- credit notes.

Periodically, the sales ledger accounts are added up and balanced for credit control purposes. It is important to record sufficient information (invoice number, credit note number, date and cash book reference) to enable the original documents (sales invoices and credit notes) or original entry (cash book) to be identified. This can be particularly handy if there is a dispute.

Other useful information will include:

- a sales ledger number;
- the customer's name, address and telephone number;
- the name of a contact at the customer's firm.

Thus a sales ledger account may take the form illustrated in Figure 11.2.

If you use a computer accounting package, sales ledger accounts are usually prepared and updated automatically when you input sales invoice, credit note and cash receipts data. It is, however, quite straightforward to prepare sales ledger accounts manually.

Accurate sales ledger accounts, along with accurate invoicing, correct deliveries and satisfactory goods, will greatly facilitate debt collection.

How can more detailed creditor information be maintained?

Accurate information should ensure that creditors are paid the right amount for goods received. As with sales, this is made possible by maintaining a separate record for each supplier. This is usually called a 'purchase ledger account'.

Sales ledger account Brown Ltd 7 Weir Lane Birdley Leics Tel No 2222 716381 Ask for P White				No 21
Date	Detail	Reference	Transaction Amount £	Balance £
01/05/01	Sales invoice	1234	560.00	560.00
10/05.01	Sales invoice	1242	220.00	780.00
15/06/01	Credit note	40	(100.00)	680.00
25/06/01	Amount received	Cash Book page 30	(460.00)	220.00

Figure 11.2   Sales ledger account

Note: transactions increasing the amount due to the business by the customer are added and those decreasing it are subtracted. The latter amounts are denoted by ( ).

When recording each transaction enter:

- date;
- detail (purchase invoice, credit note and payment);
- invoice number and credit note number;
- cash book reference.

Where necessary, this will allow the transaction to be checked. Other useful information to record in the purchase ledger account includes:

- a purchase ledger number;
- the supplier's name, address and telephone number;
- the name of a contact at the supplier's firm.

A sample purchase ledger account is given in Figure 11.3. Purchase ledger accounts can be equally well prepared either manually or by computer.

To avoid paying for unsatisfactory or unsolicited goods, only valid, accurate purchase invoices should be entered in the purchase ledger. Other invoices should be retained and queried.

Controlling and recording stock

The controlling and recording of stock is very important to home-based businesses since storage space is likely to be restricted. Also, holding stock absorbs finance.

Thus a home-based business will find it advantageous to keep stock levels at a practical minimum. To do this it is important to know the amount of stock held at any one time. Where just a few stock lines are held and stock levels are low, simple observation will provide this information. If this is not adequate you will need to consider main-taining a stock record card for each line of stock. This will record all the transactions relating to each particular line of stock and will iden-

Purchase ledger account Purple Ltd Unit 3 Table Industrial Estate Durham Tel No7777 213871 Ask for Mr A Jones				No 10
Date	Detail	Reference	Transaction Amount £	Balance £
01/03/01	Purchase invoice	2008	1,240.00	1,240.00
12/03/01	Purchase invoice	2111	750.00	1,990.00
01/04/01	Amount paid	Cash Book page 17	(1,240.00)	750.00
11/04/01	Purchase invoice	2132	800.00	1,550.00

Figure 11.3   Purchase ledger account

tify the balance of stock remaining after each transaction. An example of a stock record card is given in Figure 11.4.

Keeping day books

The preparation of the annual accounts and VAT returns can be facilitated by keeping day books for sales and purchases. The sales day book will list the sales invoices that have been issued, giving the amount inclusive of VAT, exclusive of VAT and the amount of VAT. If a busi-

Stock record card					
Stock record card No 21 Stock: White Cotton T-shirt					
Date	Detail		Quantity		
		In	Out	Balance	
21/10/01	T Waters. Goods Inwards				
	Note No 211	120		120	
22/10/01	G Hack. Despatch Note				
	Note No 428		10	110	
24/10/01	H Rub. Despatch Note				
	Note No 433		15	95	

Figure 11.4 Stock record card

ness is not registered for VAT, just the total amount of the invoice will be entered. The purchases day book will record the equivalent information for purchases and may group together purchases by type to aid analysis.

12 *The results for the year*

Why is it necessary to calculate the annual results?

Firstly, all businesses should review their financial position and results to help assess their performance. Secondly, some of this information will be required by the Inland Revenue. This task should be carried out at least once a year.

Any business operated as a limited company will, in addition to calculating the annual results, be legally required to present the information in a prescribed format.

How is the information computed?

The necessary information is prepared using two financial statements: the trading, profit and loss account and the balance sheets. The presentation of these two statements can vary but the principles behind them should be the same. An example of a balance sheet and a trading, profit and loss statement is given in Tables 12.1 and 12.2 respectively.

Table 12.1 Year end balance sheet

A balance sheet as at 30/04/01

	£	£
Fixed assets		
Motor vehicle		5,000
Current assets		
Stock	400	
Debtors	2,000	
Prepayments	150	
Cash at bank	700	
Cash in hand	50	
	3,300	
Current liabilities		
Creditors	250	
Accruals	50	
	300	
Net current assets		3,000
Long-term liabilities		
Loans		(4,000)
Net Assets		4,000
Opening capital		2,200
Add: Capital introduced during the year		1,000
Add: Profit for the year		6,800
Less: Drawings		(6,000)
Closing capital		4,000

Note: This format is suitable for a sole trader

Table 12.2   Trading, profit and loss account statement

A trading, profit and loss account statement for the year to 30/04/01

	£	£
Sales		25,000
Less: Cost of sales		(10,000)
Gross profit		15,000
Less: expenses		
Wages & salaries	5,800	
Transport	300	
Telephone	500	
Stationery	100	
Postage	100	
Advertising	400	
Sundries	200	
Depreciation	600	
Interest	200	
		(8,200)
Net profit for the year		6,800

Note: This format is suitable for a sole trader

What are the principles used to prepare the profit and loss account and the balance sheet?

There are a number of principles but we will concern ourselves with the main one used for accounts preparation. The financial statements do not record the amount of money spent or received, that is the function of the cash book. Instead they reflect what has been used and sold during the year, irrespective of whether a cash flow has taken place. This means that sales will be recorded in the financial statements for the year in which they take place (usually the year in which the delivery of goods or provision of services occurs). Any amounts due from customers at the end of the year are recorded in the balance sheet as assets.

For costs the determining factor will be usage. For example, if a large quantity of stationery is purchased during the year, only the amount used should be recorded in the trading, profit and loss account. The remainder of the stationery should be recorded as an asset in the balance sheet.

Will an accountant have to do the work?

No legal requirements exist for the year end accounts to be prepared by an accountant although, obviously, an accountant would willingly provide this service. The convenience and cost of employing an accountant have to be weighed against the time and effort required to prepare these statements yourself.

If you decide in favour of the do-it-yourself approach, many colleges offer accounting courses, and accounting kits or packages for computers are widely available.

How are these financial statements prepared?

So that the financial statements can be prepared it is essential that you keep accurate books and records all year, since these provide the information needed for the trading, profit and loss account and the balance sheet.

How to prepare the balance sheet

The balance sheet is a statement detailing the assets, liabilities and capital of a business.

Assets are the property and resources of the firm. There are two types of asset: fixed assets and current assets. Fixed assets are those assets bought for use in the business rather than for resale, and are expected to have a useful life of more than one year (possibly machinery, motor vehicles and other equipment). Current assets are those that relate to the day-to-day running of the business, such as stock, debtors, cash at the bank, cash in hand.

Liabilities represent the indebtedness of the business. Amounts due within a year are current liabilities, amounts due after one year are long-term liabilities.

The capital represents the indebtedness of the business to the owner. For accounting purposes, the business is a separate entity from the owner, and thus any resources provided by the owner are ultimately repayable.

Fixed assets

Fixed assets are recorded in the balance sheet at their cost less any depreciation that has been written off to date.

Depreciation is an allocation of the cost of a fixed asset over its useful life. For example, if a computer with a cost of £3,000 has an expected useful life of three years, depreciation could be calculated as:

$$\frac{£3,000}{3 \text{ years}} = £1,000 \text{ per annum}$$

So, at the end of the first year the computer would appear in the balance sheet at a net amount of £2,000 (£3,000 – £1,000). At the end of the second year it would appear as £1,000 (£2,000 – £1,000) and at the end of the third year it would be fully written off (£1,000 – £1,000).

Stock

The stock should be recorded in the balance sheet at its cost to the business, unless the selling price is expected to be lower (such as where items have become obsolete), in which case the selling price less any further costs should be used to value the stock. Quantities of stock are best established by counting them at the year end, a process which will not take very long for most home-based businesses. The cost of the stock can be established by referring back to the relevant purchase invoices.

Debtors

The amount owed by customers can be determined as follows:

(a)   If maintaining sales ledger cards, list and add up all the amounts outstanding on the cards at the end of the year.
(b)   Alternatively, list and add up all sales invoices unpaid at the end of the year.

If any debtors are not expected to pay, they should not be included and should be treated as an expense in the profit and loss account.

Prepayments

These are amounts paid in advance for various services, such as insurance. As an example, motor insurance of £300 paid on 31 March

2001 will be £75 prepaid (3 ÷ 12 × £300) at the year end 31 December 2001.

Cash at the bank

The amount of money at the bank can be calculated by reference to the receipts and payments recorded in the cash book. The method is outlined in Chapter 10, page 105. If the bank account is overdrawn the amount overdrawn is treated as a current liability.

Cash in hand

Simply add up any business petty cash that is held at the balance sheet date.

Creditors

The amount due to suppliers can be calculated as for sales, except that reference is made to the purchase ledger cards or unpaid purchase invoices.

Accruals

Accruals are amounts to be paid in arrears for services (for example telephone calls). Sometimes, as with telephone calls, it may be necessary to estimate the amount to be accrued at the end of the year.

Loans

The figure for loans should be the outstanding amount of capital yet to be paid. Any interest paid or payable is an expense.

Capital

The indebtedness to the owner is increased by any additional money or other property introduced by the owner and by any profit made (since this belongs to the owner). It is decreased by money or property taken by the owner as drawings. A record of money introduced and taken as drawings will be in the cash book. Capital changes caused by other events are likely to be rare unless business stock is taken for personal use. A record should be made of all such transactions.

All the assets and liabilities of the business belong to the owner; therefore, the net assets of the business are always equal to the closing capital.

How to prepare the trading, profit and loss account

The trading, profit and loss account calculates the net profit for the year.

Sales

The amount entered for sales should be the total sales made during the year. This is usually the goods despatched or the services provided during the year. The easiest way to calculate sales is to total the amount (exclusive of VAT) of all the sales invoices issued during the year. Deduct any credit notes issued; again, the amount must be net of VAT. If maintained, the sales day book will be of use in summarising the invoices for the year.

Cost of sales

The cost of sales is the sum of those costs incurred that relate directly to the sales made, for example the cost of raw materials.

Table 12.3 shows the calculation for a company that buys and sells goods.

The stock information will be provided by stock counts. Where a business is registered for VAT the purchases can be calculated by adding up the amounts (excluding VAT) from the year's invoices that relate to purchase of stock, and deducting any relevant debit notes

Table 12.3 Cost of sales for a company buying and selling goods

	£
Opening stock	500
Add: Purchases (stock bought during the year)	2,300
Less: Closing stock	(400)
Cost of sales	2,400

(excluding VAT). Where a firm is not registered, the amounts including VAT should be used. If prepared, a purchase day book will help this process.

Table 12.4 shows the calculation for a company that provides a service.

Table 12.4 Cost of sales for a company providing a service

	£
Opening stock (including work in progress)	2,100
Add: Purchases	200
Add: Labour	5,000
Less: Closing stock (including work in progress)	(900)
Cost of sales	6,400

Any work-in-progress amounts can be ascertained by reference to time records or diaries. Other stocks can be counted. The labour costs should include only those that relate directly to providing the service. Details should be available from time records or diaries.

Table 12.5 shows the cost of sales for a business that manufacturers and sells goods.

Table 12.5 Cost of sales for a company that manufacturers and sells goods

	£
Opening stock	700
Add: Purchases	4,000
Add: Labour	3,000
Add: Manufacturing overheads	1,200
Less: Closing stock	(800)
Cost of sales	8,100

The stock figures should include all types of stock – raw materials, work in progress and finished goods – and should be ascertained by stock counts. Purchases are calculated as previously explained.

The cost-of-labour figure represents the wages incurred in manufacturing the items to be sold. This can be ascertained as previously outlined.

Manufacturing overheads are computed in the same way as other expenses, a point which is explained in the next section. They include supervisory wages and power. For home-based manufacturing businesses overheads are likely to be low.

Expenses

Expenses are the assets or benefits that have been used up in a business in achieving the sales. It is, therefore, important to calculate the usage, not the amount paid. As an illustration, an advertisement in a newspaper may be paid for before the year end, say 31/12/01, but the advertisement appears only after the year end. In this case the expense of the advertisement should be recorded in the accounts for the year ended 31/12/02. On the other hand, telephone calls made before the end of the year 31/12/01 may not become payable until the following year (due to the nature of BT invoicing). However, the cost of such calls should be included as an expense of the year ending 31/12/01.

Deprecation

Deprecation is calculated on a different basis from other expenses. Depreciation is an allocation of the cost of fixed assets over their useful lives (in other words an estimate of their usage). If a car with an initial cost of £6,000 has an expected useful life of three years, depreciation could be calculated to be:

$$\frac{£6,000}{3 \text{ years}} = £2,000 \text{ pa}$$

Therefore, each year, for three years, a depreciation expense of £2,000 would be recorded in the profit statement.

What about partnership accounts?

Partnership accounts are of the same format as those for a sole trader except that both the profit shared between partners and their portion of the capital is shown.

What about limited companies?

There are additional rules and regulations relating to the accounts of a limited company. These are quite detailed and lengthy. To comply with these rules and regulations is a legal requirement.

The preparation of the accounts of a limited company requires the services of an accountant or similarly trained and experienced person. They may also need to be audited.

Private expenses

Any amounts paid for private expenses should be excluded from the accounts as they are not genuine business expenditure. Where there are expenses that relate partly to the business and partly to the owner's private use the expenses should be fairly apportioned between the two. This is particularly relevant to the home-based business, as expenses such as the telephone, motor car, heating and light often fall into this category. If you do not calculate a fair proportion in your accounts, the Inland Revenue will certainly do it for you, most probably on a less generous basis. You must be able to justify the rates of apportionment you apply.

For example:

Heat and light. The amount of heat and light charged to the business could be based on the area of the home used for the business. If your office is 10 per cent of your home it would be reasonable to charge 10 per cent of your gas and electricity bills to the business.

Motor expenses. These can be based on the ratio of business to private miles travelled. A record of all business trips should be kept.

Telephone calls. These are a little more difficult to judge. Itemised billing, now available from most suppliers, can help. As an alternative, keep a record of business calls and private calls to estimate the proportion of business to private telephone expenses.

If your spouse, who is not a business partner, helps you with your business, perhaps by taking telephone messages, it is quite acceptable to pay him or her a salary. This can be advantageous in taxation terms if your spouse would not otherwise use up his or her full tax allowance.

13 *Rules and regulations*

There are vast numbers of rules and regulations that apply to the home-based business. Some of these are discussed in other chapters, for example under taxation, VAT and insurance. The remaining areas of concern to the home-based business entrepreneur are dealt with in this chapter and include:

- planning permission;
- copyright and patents;
- the Data Protection Act;
- business names;
- limited company requirement;
- health and safety;
- consumer legislation;
- food safety;
- disclosure of information on business stationery.

Other legal constraints may be applicable, depending upon the nature of the business. Many trades form associations, institutes or societies and to join, you are usually required to give an undertaking to abide by the rules of the governing body. These rules usually represent best practice.

Planning permission

Planning permission is not normally required unless material changes to the character or usage of the dwelling place are intended. Home-based businesses will be allowed to trade provided they do not cause any inconvenience to their neighbours. Contact the planning officer at your local council offices for further help and advice. In any decision, they will consider whether the noise, traffic or fumes generated will affect the local area.

Copyright and patents

When planning to use material such as text, patterns, photographs, pictures and so forth that belong to someone else, it is important not to infringe copyright or patent.

A patent is a document that will secure exclusive rights for the person who registers a new invention. If you have such an invention you should register it with:

> The Patent Office
> Concept House
> Cardiff Road
> Newport
> South Wales NP10 8QQ

This will protect it from being copied. If you do not have an invention you may not, without permission, copy others that have been patented. The Patent Office and the Science Reference Library can be contacted at the above address to establish whether or not a patent already exists. The telephone number for the central enquiry unit is: 08459 500 505.

Copyright is the exclusive right to use such items as written text, paintings, photographs, designs, patterns and music. Copyright is automatic and is usually with the person who created or produced the work, although it is possible to sell the copyright to others.

You may not use work that is subject to copyright unless you have first obtained permission. If you are in any doubt about whether you have or are likely to infringe someone else's copyright you would be wise to consult a solicitor.

Manufactured goods are also protected in a similar way to copyright. This protection is known as the unregistered design right. In most cases it lasts for only 10 years after first marketing the article (subject to an overall limit of 15 years from its creation), after which the item can be copied or imitated.

The Data Protection Act

The Data Protection Act could affect anyone publishing information about people. It is a legal requirement to check with the Data Protection Registrar whether you need to be registered. Contact:

> The Data Protection Registrar
> Wycliffe House
> Water Lane
> Wilmslow
> Cheshire SK9 5AF
> Tel: 01625 545745

For more information, visit www.dataprotection.gov.uk

Business names

It is worth spending some time deciding on a suitable name for your business. After all, you want it to be memorable and convey an appropriate image.

Limited company names

All limited company names must be registered with the Registrar of

Companies at the address given on page 18. Before being accepted for registration a company name will be scrutinised to make sure that:

- It is not the same as a name already registered.
- The word 'Limited' or the abbreviation 'Ltd' is included at the end of the name. Welsh and Scottish Gaelic equivalents can be used.
- It is not offensive.
- It is not the same as (or very similar to) a name already on the index.

Special permission is needed to use certain words or phrases. In general, these are words or expressions that imply that the company has a certain standing. They include:

- British (and similar).
- Association (and similar).
- Royal (and similar).
- Charity.
- University.
- Nurse, nursing.
- Institute.
- Group.
- Foundation.
- Benevolent.
- Council (and similar).
- Charter (or Chartered).
- Trust.

Further assistance can be obtained from the Registrar or Companies.

Non-limited company names

Non-incorporated businesses do not have to register their name. None the less, it is incumbent upon them to choose a name that cannot be confused with that of another business. There are also restrictions on the use of such words as Royal, British, and the other restricted use words given above. The Department of Trade and Industry will help you with this. In addition, you should ensure that the selected name does not infringe any trade marks by requesting a search from:

> The Trade Marks Registry
> Patent Office
> Concept House
> Cardiff Road
> Newport
> South Wales NP10 8QQ
> Tel: 08459 500 505
> E-mail: enquiries@patent.gov.uk
> Web site: www.patent.gov.uk

Domain names

If you are considering a Web presence for your business, now or in the future, then you will need to consider obtaining a domain name. Many businesses like their domain name to reflect the nature and/or the name of the business, as this is easier for their customers to remember. The availability of a suitable domain name should therefore be considered at the same time as choosing your business name.

Limited company requirements

Limited companies must be legally formed and registered. This is best done by a solicitor or a business specialising in this area (a registration agent). Limited company status provides useful limited liability for the shareholders, but there is a price to pay for this protection which includes:

- An annual general meeting may be necessary.
- An audit will be necessary for many companies, but most of those with a turnover of not more than £1 million and with a balance sheet total of not more than £1.4 million are exempt.
- A set of annual accounts must be prepared to a prescribed format. These must be filed with the Registrar of Companies. There are some exemptions for small limited companies.
- An annual return form must be prepared.
- The Registrar of Companies must be notified of any changes to the company, such as a change of directors.
- An annual registration fee must be paid.
- A register of directors must be maintained.
- Certain books and records must be available for inspection at the company's registered office (this can be your home address or a solicitor's office, for example).

A company should not act outside the scope of its memorandum and articles of association. These important documents, prepared when the company is formed, outline what the company may and may not do. Therefore, the scope of company activities should be thought out beforehand. These documents can be revised but this is best done after sound legal advice.

The directors of a company have certain obligations. They are responsible for ensuring that their company operates within the law, particularly the Companies Act. They should ensure that all relevant documents are correctly prepared and delivered to the Registrar of Companies by the due date. These will include the annual return and the accounts. Directors are responsible for the day-to-day running of the company's affairs and must not allow it to trade if it is insolvent.

The company secretary will be responsible for maintaining the company registers (for example, the register of directors).

Health and safety

The area of health and safety is covered by the Health and Safety Executive (HSE) and your local Environmental Health Department. In general, the HSE will deal with hazardous businesses such as manu-facturing and transport, and the Environmental Health with catering, hotels, hairdressers and retail, to name but a few.

The Health and Safety Act applies to all places of work, but if you work for yourself, with no employees, you may not need to register. You are, therefore, unlikely to be affected by the Act unless your neighbours complain. Still, it is sensible to provide yourself with a safe working environment. If you do employ staff, health and safety regula-tions will apply and it will be necessary to contact the HSE and Environmental Health to find out which rules will affect you. Compliance with many of the rules will just require common sense. Child minders, for example, will probably require fireguards, stair gates and secure garden gates before they can be registered with the local authority.

Contact the HSE information line on 08701 545500 or e-mail hseinformationservices@natbrit.com to find out which regulations will apply to you.

Consumer legislation

There are a number of Acts of Parliament governing the sale of goods and services. A summary of the main legislation is given below:

- The goods should accurately match their description, whether it is written or not.
- The goods must be of merchantable quality. They must, there-fore, work properly, be in satisfactory condition, be free from minor defects and last for a reasonable period of time. Goods must be safe.

- The goods must be suitable for any purpose for which they are purchased if this has been indicated by the vendor.

If the above rules are broken, provided the goods are returned promptly, the purchaser can claim for the full purchase price and any directly resulting loss or damage.

- If, prior to purchase, faults or defects are pointed out to the buyer or if the buyer examines the goods and accepts the faults or defects, a claim for poor quality or faulty goods is likely to be unsuccessful.
- Goods supplied on hire, or in part exchange, must meet the same criteria as goods bought and sold.
- Whether there is a fixed agreement or not, a customer is entitled to expect a service to be performed with reasonable care and skill within a reasonable time. What constitutes 'reasonable' is usually established by reference to what would be expected of a competent member of the relevant profession.
- There is no legal obligation to give a refund or an exchange of goods where the buyer has simply changed his or her mind.
- It is a criminal offence to sell items which are falsely described or unsafe. It is also a criminal offence to give a misleading price indication.

Advice in this area is available from your local Trading Standards Office, or from:

> The Office of Fair Trading
> Fleetbank House
> 2–6 Salisbury Square
> London EC4Y 8JX
> Tel: 08457 224499
> E-mail: enquiries@oft.gov.uk
> Web site: www.oft.gov.uk

Croner's reference books offer a number of publications suitable for the self-employed and smaller businesses. Contact:

> Croner Publications
> 145 London Road
> Kingston-upon-Thames
> Surrey KT2 6SR
> Tel: 020 8547 3333
> E-mail: info@croner.co.uk

The Consumer Affairs Division of the Department of Trade and Industry, a further source of advice, can be contacted at:

> Department of Trade and Industry
> 1 Victoria Street
> London SW1H 0ET
> Tel: 020 7215 5000

The DTI Web site, www.dti.go.uk, gives useful information and contact details about consumer affairs, employment, business support and Business Link.

Food safety

Any business (including home-based ones) dealing with food will need to abide by the Food Safety Act. The Act requires that staff dealing with food be suitably trained in food hygiene (courses are provided at local colleges) and lays down regulations about the preparation and storage of food. If you wish to prepare food in your home for sale to the public you may have to register with your local Environmental Services Department. It may be necessary to modify your own kitchen before it can be used for food preparation or storage.

Disclosure of information on business stationery

The following information, as appropriate, must be shown clearly on invoices, receipts, letters, purchase orders and written demands for the payment of business debts:

- the name of the sole trader;
- the names of each partner;
- the name of the company;
- an address for each person named where documents can be served.

14 Dealing with the Inland Revenue

What is the Inland Revenue?

The Inland Revenue is the government department that administers and collects most forms of taxation. Your local tax office will be happy to discuss any problems or questions that you have and will offer advice and explanations.

When should I contact the Inland Revenue?

You should notify your local tax office as soon as you start business. The address and telephone number can be found in your local telephone directory. The Inland Revenue will provide information and help before you commence trading. It also deals with National Insurance contributions (NIC) (see Chapter 16, page 165).

Once you have been allotted a reference number, quote it each time you contact your tax office.

Is it beneficial to employ an accountant?

There is no requirement to employ an accountant. The Inland Revenue will accept information and tax computations prepared by you.

Where a home-based business has few taxation complications and few changes from year to year the owner should consider dealing with his or her own tax affairs. Under these circumstances, with a little advice from the tax office, it should be possible to produce the relevant information without too much time and effort. If you send in your tax return before 30 September of the relevant year (ie 30 September 2002 for the tax year ending 6 April 2002), the Inland Revenue will calculate your tax for you.

If your tax affairs are more complex, employing an accountant may be essential. Although accountants charge fees for their services it can be money well spent if it releases more time for you to manage your business. In any event, an accountant may be able to identify tax savings which could at least partly offset the fees.

Whether you are preparing your own tax affairs or drawing together information for a tax accountant to use, annual tax booklets such as *Whillan's Tax Tables* will be very useful, and cost only a few pounds.

What types of taxation are there?

Almost all home-based business entrepreneurs will need to calculate and pay tax. This might be pay as you earn (PAYE) or taxation of business profits. It is also possible that some business owners will be affected, at some time, by capital gains tax.

Companies will also have to account for corporation tax. For taxation purposes companies are treated as separate legal entities.

Pay as you earn (PAYE)

PAYE is the method used to collect income tax from employees (this includes company directors). The tax is collected each month or each week by the employer, who has then to pay it to the Inland Revenue. The amount of PAYE is calculated by reference to tables and other information provided by the Inland Revenue. Alternatively, there are suitable computer packages that can do the calculations. If you employ staff you will be required to operate a PAYE system. In cases where the employees' salaries are below a certain level there are reduced PAYE requirements. When you are considering employing staff contact your local tax office who will provide you with an information pack and answer any questions.

Employed or self-employed?

When deciding whether to tax a person as an employee or self-employed the Inland Revenue will evaluate the nature of the work and how it is carried out. A person who is remunerated hourly, weekly or monthly, can be paid overtime, works set hours and works at premises determined by the person he or she works for, is likely to be an employee. Someone who risks capital in the business, usually provides the necessary equipment and has to carry out any remedial work in his or her own time and at his or her own expense, will probably be deemed to be self-employed. The Inland Revenue has leaflets offering guidance.

A self-employed person will be able to deduct from his or her income expenses which are incurred in the course of business in order to earn a profit. The net amount (the business profits) will be treated as income for the year and be assessed for tax purposes. An employee is much more limited in the deductions that can be made from gross income.

IR 35

Until recently, it has been possible to avoid the debate over registering as self-employed or employed by operating as a limited company. IR 35 now limits the advantages of this method of operation if the true nature of the arrangement is that of an employee working for an employer. In such a case, a company may find itself paying more tax and national insurance than previously. Contact your local tax office if you feel this may apply to you

Taxation of business profits

The profits of a business (not a limited company) are taxed as part of the income of the business's owner. Profits, under the taxation rules, may be different from those calculated under the accounting rules outlined in Chapter 12. Taxation rules are covered in more detail throughout this chapter.

This taxation is payable on the profits of any business whether operated on a full-time, part-time, or spare-time basis, and even includes profitable hobbies.

Capital gains tax

Capital gains tax may arise on the disposal, often, but not necessarily, the sale of certain capital items such as shares and machinery. In general, the gain is calculated by deducting the cost of the asset disposed of from the sale proceeds. The gain calculated may be further reduced by the indexation allowance and taper relief.

There are two main ways in which home-based business owners can become liable for capital gains tax as a result of their business activities.

The first arises if the business, or the assets in it, are sold. There are complex rules in this area but there may be some relief from capital gains tax if the proceeds of the disposal are reinvested in another similar business. Where the proceeds are not reinvested, and the reason for the disposal is retirement due to age or ill-health, relieve may be available.

Use of the home for business purposes can, under certain circumstances, lead to a chargeable capital gain when the home is sold. If part of your home is used exclusively for business purpose a charge could arise. Many home-based businesses do not fall into this category; while you may use your kitchen table for your business activities, it is also used for other purposes. The same applies to a spare bedroom which you might also use as an office.

Each person (but not companies) has a capital gains allowance. Only when capital gains, in any one year, exceed this allowance does tax become payable. The annual amount of the capital gains allowance for the tax year 2001/2002 is £7,500.

Corporation tax

This is payable on the profits made by a company. As with the taxation of business profits, the profits for taxation purposes may vary from those calculated for accounting purposes. Corporation tax is payable by the company, not the owners.

How much income tax will I have to pay?

The amount of income tax paid by an individual depends upon his or her personal circumstances. Tax is paid on the net amount of all income after subtracting any allowable deductions and allowances. This is known as 'taxable income'. The rate of tax depends upon the level of taxable income. For the tax year 2001/2002 the rates are 10 per cent on the first £1,850, 22 per cent on the next £27,520 and 40 per cent thereafter. These bands are liable to change, however, with each new Budget.

Income includes:

- profits from the business;
- salaries;
- dividends;
- interest received (for example from building societies).

Allowable deductions include pension contributions approved by the Inland Revenue, retirement annuity premiums and some types of loan interest.

The main allowance is the basic allowance, which is £4,535 for the tax year 2001/2002. A child tax credit has also been introduced for this year.

The rate of capital gains tax will depend upon the level of taxable income of the individual. The capital gains will be assessed according to the banding for income tax, starting where the taxable income finished. It could thus be 10 per cent, 22 per cent or 40 per cent.

If you are a director paying PAYE your estimated tax for the year, based on your annual income tax return, will be collected monthly or weekly as for any other employee.

The regulations and rates of taxation are regularly reviewed, changes being announced in the Budget.

How are taxable profits calculated?

Taxable profits (prepared under the taxation rules) and accounting profits (prepared using the accounting rules, some of which are outlined in Chapter 12 are often different amounts. The starting point for calculating taxable profits is the profit as calculated in the trading, profit and loss account. This amount is then altered to account for the variations between taxation and accounting rules.

The main variation arises as a result of the regulations governing fixed assets. Accounting profits are calculated by making an allowance for depreciation on fixed assets (see Chapter 12). However, depreciation is not a tax deductible expense. Instead, the Inland Revenue calculates a capital allowance for fixed assets. The allowance is usually 25 per cent of any currently unclaimed balance of capital items.

Capital allowances are available on such items as vans, cars (but only on the portion used for business), furniture, computers and ladders. An allowance of 100 per cent is currently allowed on some software, computers and similar items.

Also, any amounts paid for private expenses and some entertaining expenses are not allowable against tax and should be excluded from the accounts.

In summary, a simple tax computation might look like Table 14.1.

Table 14.1 Calculating tax

	£
Profits as per accounts	10,000
(excluding private transactions and use of assets)	
Add back:	
Deprecation	1,000
Entertaining expenses	200
Less:	
Capital allowances	(800)
Taxable profit	10,400

What books and records are required?

The books and records suggested in Chapter 10 and 11 should provide sufficient information for taxation purposes. Whichever books and records you opt for should provide the following information:

- amounts received;
- amounts spent and on what (see Inland Revenue literature for the categories of expenditure recommended);
- the amounts of capital introduced and from whence it came (possibly savings or dividends);
- the amount of any money drawn for the owner's use or any cheques paid on the owner's behalf;
- the market value of any goods taken from the business for a non-business use.

All books and records should be retained as evidence of the figures in your accounts. The burden of proof is on the taxpayer, not the Inland Revenue.

How is a partnership taxed?

Once tax assessment is made on the profits of the partnership as a whole (prepared on a basis similar to that of a sole trader business), the amount is shared out among the partners. Their tax liability will also be based on their personal circumstances.

A change in partners will result in the business being taxed as though the partnership ceases to trade and then starts up again as a new business. A capital gains liability could arise.

How is a limited company taxed?

Limited companies pay corporation tax on their taxable profits for the year. These profits are calculated on a basis similar to that of a sole trader. However, directors' salaries are a deductible business expense whereas that of a sole trader is not. The rate of corporation tax varies depending upon the level of profits. For companies with profits of £10,000 or less, it is 10 per cent.

Directors of the company (often the shareholders) are treated as employees and taxed under the PAYE system. Where the directors (and other employees) are deemed to have enjoyed a benefit in kind, such as a company car, they become liable to an increased income tax bill. The rules for benefits in kind are quite complicated and you may wish to read the relevant Inland Revenue literature and then discuss them with your accountant or the Inland Revenue.

When is tax payable?

In general, the payment dates are as follows:

- Tax and National Insurance contributions collected under the PAYE scheme are payable on the 19th day of the month following the month to which the deductions relate. Where the payments average out at less than £1,500, payments can be made quarterly.
- Corporation tax is usually payable nine months after the company's year end.
- Capital gains tax is payable on 31 January.
- Tax on business profits is payable in three instalments. Two estimated instalments are paid on 31 January and 31 July, a final settlement being made on 31 January of the following year.

As the taxation (except under the PAYE scheme) is payable in arrears, it is important, in order to avoid a large tax bill which you can't pay, to put regular amounts aside.

What is a self-assessment?

Since 1997, taxpayers have been responsible for calculating their own tax liability. However, where tax returns are received by the Inland

Revenue on or before 30 September following the end of the tax year (eg 30 September 2002 for the tax year to 5 April 2002), the Inland Revenue will calculate the tax liability if desired.

This chapter covers the tax regulations most applicable to the home-based business. However, it represents just a few of the tax regulations in existence and should not be relied on as a comprehensive guide. Tax regulations are subject to change by the government of the day.

15　Dealing with HM Customs and Excise

What is HM Customs and Excise?

HM Customs and Excise is the government department that administers and collects Value Added Tax (VAT). If you have any problems or queries regarding VAT, Customs and Excise officials are happy to offer free help and advice. After all, it is in their interests that you get your VAT returns right. Customs and Excise issues a number of leaflets covering all aspects of VAT which are available on request.

What is VAT?

VAT is an indirect tax on consumer expenditure on most goods and services. The VAT is collected by those businesses or people providing the goods or services.

A typical business registered for VAT will pay VAT on many of its purchases and charge VAT on its sales. Any VAT paid can be offset against any VAT collected from customers. The net amount will be paid to or refunded by Customs and Excise as appropriate.

Will it be necessary to register for VAT?

All businesses with taxable supplies (such as sales) in excess of, or expected to be in excess of, the pre-set limit for any 12-month period must register for VAT. The limit is reviewed at each Budget. It is currently £54,000.

Other businesses may, in general, register if they wish. Voluntary registration could be advantageous for a trader who expects repayments from Customs and Excise (such as where some outputs relate to zero-rated or exempt supplies). The drawbacks are the increase in administrative work and the effect of charging VAT to customers.

In some industries, the building trade for example, VAT registration can improve a firm's credibility.

What are taxable supplies?

In the main a taxable supply is the provision of goods or services to customers, in other words the sales of the business. Other taxable supplies include:

- goods taken from the business for private use;
- hire of goods to someone;
- some gifts;
- disposal of some business assets.

What is output VAT?

This is VAT charged on taxable supplies.

What is input VAT?

This is the VAT that is charged on business purchases and expenses and includes:

- the purchase of goods;
- the purchase of services.

Some items are specifically excluded, such as:

- the purchase of a car;
- business entertainment;
- goods or services for private use.

When should I contact Customs and Excise?

You can contact Customs and Excise whenever you encounter a problem with VAT. Customs and Excise will be willing to advise you. The telephone number of you local office is in the telephone directory. When writing or telephoning, quote your VAT registration number and any other reference number. This will speed up any enquiries.

If you receive advice on VAT matters via the telephone, send a letter confirming and explaining your request for help and ask that their reply is confirmed in writing. This will ensure that you have fully understood the advice and the written reply can act as evidence should there be a dispute later. Disputes can arise because VAT officers vary in their interpretation of the rules.

How is VAT calculated?

There are, currently, three VAT rates: a standard rate of 17½ per cent, a reduced rate of 5 per cent and a zero rate (nil). Obviously, no calculation is required if the zero rate is applied. The reduced rate relates to domestic fuel and power. The following examples illustrate how to calculate VAT at 17½ per cent.

Example 1

	£
Total invoice value of goods or services before VAT	200
VAT @ 17½%	

Or 17.5

$$\frac{17.5}{100} \times 200 = \qquad 35$$

Total inclusive of VAT	235

The customer should therefore be charged £235, £35 of this being due to Customs and Excise, and the supplier retaining £200.

Example 2

If the value of the goods or services exclusive of VAT is not known, the amount of VAT can be calculated as follows:

	£
Amount inclusive of VAT	235
VAT @ 17½%	

$$\frac{17.5}{117.5} \times 235 = \qquad 35$$

Amount exclusive of VAT	200

The VAT rate and the rules and regulations associated with VAT are changed from time to time. These alterations are announced in the Budget. In recent years there have been a number of changes to help small businesses, so home-based business entrepreneurs would be well advised to keep abreast of developments.

Which VAT rate will be applicable?

As mentioned above, there are three rates of VAT, the standard rate, which is currently 17½ per cent, the reduced rate, and the zero rate. However, some goods are exempt from VAT. Exempt goods include:

- some betting, gaming and lotteries;
- some education and training.

Zero-rated items include:

- most food and drink, but not the provision of food as a service, such as in a restaurant;
- books, magazines and newspapers;
- shoes and clothes for small children.

Exempt and zero-rated items are in a small minority. A list is available from Customs and Excise. The vast majority of items are at standard rate. If you provide only exempt good or services you cannot be registered for VAT.

How is the amount of VAT due to or from Customs and Excise calculated?

Input VAT (that paid to suppliers) can be deducted from output VAT (that collected from customers) and the net amount paid to Customs and Excise. If input VAT is more than output VAT the net amount can be reclaimed from Customs and Excise. The majority of home-based businesses will be in the position of making net payments.

Usually, the calculation of VAT payable or reclaimable is made every three months (quarterly) by completing a VAT return; the quarter-end date will be determined by Customs and Excise. This form has to be returned to Customs and Excise, together with any payment, within 30 days of the quarter end. If you expect repayments of tax it is possible to register for monthly returns and thus monthly repayments, boosting your cash flow.

The annual accounting and cash accounting VAT schemes

Small businesses (currently those with taxable supplies, excluding VAT, of less than £600,000), can apply to join the annual accounting scheme. This involves one annual return and several estimated payments (by direct debit).

There are two bases for identifying in which VAT period transactions fall. The VAT return can be based on the tax date of those invoices issued and received or on the basis of payments made and received. Alternatively, the VAT return can be calculated through the cash accounting scheme.

This scheme is again available only where taxable supplies (exclusive of VAT) are less than £600,000. This amount, of course, is subject to constant review and changes are announced in the Budget. It is designed to help the cash flow of small businesses who will have to account for output and input VAT only when it has been received or paid.

To be accepted for the scheme you must have books and records capable of identifying when the purchase invoices are paid and sales invoice monies are received. You must also have a good record as far as your dealings with Customs and Excise are concerned.

The cash accounting scheme may not be beneficial to those businesses that expect a repayment of VAT or are usually paid as soon as a sale is made.

What records are required for VAT purposes?

The books and records illustrated in Chapters 10 and 11 should provide the information necessary for the majority of home-based firms. The main information required to prepare a VAT return is listed below.

The amount of VAT due on sales and other outputs

If you are using the cash accounting scheme this amount will be available from the cash book. If not, the amount must be based on the sales invoices issued. This can be prepared by adding up the VAT on sales invoices issued or is available from the sales day book if one is maintained. Any VAT on credit notes should be deducted from the invoice and sales day book totals.

The amount of input VAT that is reclaimable

As for outputs, the source of this information will vary depending on the nature of the VAT scheme and the books that are kept. Select the most appropriate from:

● the cash book;
● the day book;
● invoices.

Any VAT on debit notes should be deducted from invoice and day book totals.

Input VAT can be reclaimed only where the purchases are for the business and a valid tax invoice retained. There are a number of notable exemptions. For example, VAT cannot usually be reclaimed on:

● cars;
● business entertainment expenses;
● certain items installed in buildings.

The total of outputs exclusive of VAT

This can either be found by reference to the cash book, by totalling the sales invoices, or by reference to the sales day book. Where there are credit notes, the amount, exclusive of VAT, should be deducted from the total of invoices or the day book total.

Other outputs such as the sale of fixed assets will be available from the cash book.

The value of total inputs exclusive of VAT

Again, this can be found by reference to the cash book, invoices or day books. The invoice and day book totals should be net of any debit notes. Do not include items such as wages and salaries, PAYE and National Insurance, loans and capital.

Keep your VAT records

A record of the amounts used in the VAT return, where they came from and to what they relate (for example which invoices) should be kept. For VAT purposes all relevant records must be kept for six years. These include:

- sales invoices;
- purchase invoices;
- cash books;
- any other accounting books (such as sales day books);
- bank statements, cheque book counterfoils and paying-in slips;
- orders;
- delivery documents;
- a VAT account.

What happens if I make a mistake?

It is best to admit your error. Mistakes will be viewed more favourably if they are found and reported by you. If the net amount of errors identified is more than £2,000 you should send a written notification of the mistakes to your local VAT office. The letter should list each error, indicating how it arose and whether it resulted in an under- or over-declaration of tax. Where the mistakes resulted in an under declaration of VAT you will be charged interest, so send a cheque to Customs and Excise as soon as possible to minimise interest charges.

If the net amount of errors is less than £2,000 it can be disclosed on the VAT return. No interest will be charged. Serious errors could result in a financial penalty as well as interest charges.

Can a computer be used?

Yes, a suitable computer package will calculate and record VAT on all relevant purchases and sales at the push of a button. It will also summarise the information for the VAT return.

Before installing a computer program, you should contact your local VAT office to ensure that your chosen software provides sufficient VAT information. If it does not, you will have to change to another program or modify the one you have until it does supply the required information.

Keep up to date

This chapter looks at VAT and how it affects many home-based businesses. It provides a guide to the most common aspects, but before you deal with your VAT all Customs and Excise literature should be reviewed to identify any other requirements that are applicable or any changes to the regulations.

16

Dealing with other people

With whom will I have to deal?

A home-based entrepreneur has to deal with a variety of people, such as the officers of the Inland Revenue and HM Customs and Excise, which have been discussed in Chapters 14 and 15.

Others you may have contact with are:

- accountants;
- solicitors;
- bank employees;
- other business advisers such as your local Business Link;
- suppliers;
- customers;
- employees.

How should I deal with these people?

There can be no fixed rules since everyone is different. It is therefore important to 'play things by ear'. However, some universally useful rules are:

- Be polite and do not lose your temper.
- Be professional; this will generate confidence.
- Use names where possible; keeping an up-to-date record will help.
- Be punctual, concise and don't waste people's time.
- Wherever practicable, use the written word. This has the advantage of providing a documentary record of communications.
- Always answer your telephone politely – you never know who may be calling.

Accountants

There are various types of accountants and bookkeepers. Anyone can call him- or herself an accountant (although many will be qualified) or bookkeeper, so be careful who you choose to do your work. If possible obtain personal recommendations. Find out about the qualifications and experience of anyone you intend to employ in this capacity. Membership of an accounting body, such as the Institute of Chartered Accountants (the accountant's name will be followed by the letters FCA or ACA), indicates that the accountant has qualifications and experience and adheres to the body's code of professional ethics. An accountant is likely to be able to offer a wider range of services but a bookkeeper may be able to do all that is required for many home-based businesses. Discuss your current and likely future needs before employing anyone.

Accountancy fees can vary enormously and it will pay to shop around. Obtain a number of written quotes but remember to be honest about the state of your books and records, or you could end up paying more than you intended. Many accountancy professionals charge by the hour, so any mistakes you make will cost you money. If you believe the quotes you receive are too high, ask for a bill breakdown and how it could be reduced. For example, you could add up your own books and records. Ask for a letter of engagement outlining the services to be provided. This can prevent arguments at a later date.

Once the accounting work has been completed make sure you understand the figures, the results for the year and the bill; if not, discuss them with your accountant or bookkeeper until you are satisfied. Find out if your books and records could be improved and if so, how.

If you are operating your business as a limited company you may also require an auditor. Only qualified chartered and certified accountants can act as auditors.

Accountants and bookkeepers will be listed in the local press or *Yellow Pages*.

Solicitors

Local lawyers can be looked up in the *Yellow Pages*. If possible, engage someone who has been personally recommended. Most solicitors are able to deal with normal business problems such as the collection of bad debts, contracts of employment and other such business contracts, but some of the more complex areas, such as the Trade Descriptions Act, patents and copyright are best dealt with by solicitors specialising in those subjects.

Before placing any work with a solicitor ask for a written quote. If you are not happy with the amount, discuss it with the solicitor to discover why the work appears expensive. If you are still not satisfied obtain further quotes.

The bank

Banks are able to provide a useful source of help for anyone either starting or running their own business. Speak to the local branch of your bank and find out about the range of support they have available.

Quite often, the bank will be able to help you prepare a business plan, which will help you get off to the best of starts. In addition to providing current accounts, loans and overdrafts, they can also provide you with a range of other services that not only save you time and money, but also allow you to get on with the main task at hand – running your business.

If you do intend to borrow money from a bank, take care to understand the terms and conditions relating to any overdraft or loan. Ask your bank manager to go through all terms and charges with you. Also, it is a good idea to consult a solicitor for advice, particularly where a large sum of money or security is involved.

Other business advisers

Advisers such as Business Links, Jobcentres and enterprise agencies are there to help. You enhance you chances of receiving useful advice if you:

- state your problem clearly;
- listen carefully to the information you are given and ask appropriate questions;
- behave politely to the people providing advice;
- show interest in their advice;
- take note of any recommendations they may make;
- do a little research before meeting the advisers – there may then be less information to take in all at once;
- realise that advisers are just that; they give advice and information, they cannot necessarily resolve your business problems;
- keep a record of you conversations so that important facts are not forgotten or misinterpreted.

Working out your National Insurance contributions (NICs)

The Inland Revenue is the government department responsible for National Insurance contributions (NICs). You will be responsible for paying your own NIC and those of any employees together with employers' National Insurance. This is in addition to the salaries and wages you pay to your staff. The Inland Revenue should be contacted as soon as you commence trading.

Employees, (including directors), earning sufficient salary, pay national insurance contributions on a monthly or weekly basis, the amount being calculated from tables supplied to you by the Inland Revenue or by a suitable computer package if you have one. The amount is payable by the 19th day of the month following that in which the deductions are made.

If you are a partner or a sole trader you will be required to pay a flat rate Class 2 NIC of £2.00 per week (2001/02) and possibly a Class 4 NIC. The latter is based on the level of your profits. However, these profits can differ from both accounting and taxable profits. The main differences are that personal tax allowances and pension-related payments are not deducted before the calculation for Class 4 NIC is made. Class 4 NIC is calculated as 7 per cent of profits between £4,535 and £29,900. Class 2 NIC is paid on a regular basis. Class 4 NIC is assessed at the same time as taxable profits. These figures can change with each Budget. Currently (2001/2002), if your profit is below £3,955, you can apply for an exemption from paying Class 2 NIC, but weigh up this saving against the benefits you would lose.

Suppliers

Being on good terms with your suppliers can be useful. A valued customer is more likely to receive good service than one who does not pay on time and who is rude and awkward. Keep a record of contacts so that you can ask for them by name. This can speed up your dealings with your suppliers and will help you to maintain friendly relations. Make sure that your bookkeeping system is efficient, otherwise you may get a reputation for being unprofessional or, worse, a bad payer.

Customers

Much of how to deal with customers has been covered in Chapters 6 and 8. It is essential to maintain good relations with customers, so keep a record of conversations and agreements as this will ensure that you do not appear to have forgotten important facts. A good, up-to-date, bookkeeping system will enable you to invoice your customers for the correct amount and ask for payment only when it falls due.

Employees

A good employee is a valuable business resource. It is, therefore, worth taking steps to locate, train and retain skilful, amiable and trustworthy staff. Before recruiting staff it is advisable to decide:

- The skills and experience you require, dividing them up into the essential and the desirable.
- What training you are prepared to offer.
- The personal qualities necessary both for the job itself and fitting in with you and the rest of your workforce.
- On a job description so that both you and potential employees are clear about the nature of the job. It is a waste of everyone's time and effort if an employee leaves shortly after employment because of a misunderstanding over job content.
- The range of salary you are prepared to offer.

The vacancy could be advertised in the local press, trade press, at the Jobcentre or in a newsagent's window. An employment agency may also be able to help, but a charge is made.

Your advertisement must not discriminate on the grounds of either race or sex.

If you expect a large number of applicants it is advisable to ask them to submit a curriculum vitae (CV) or letter outlining their qualifications and experience. This will help you to select the best candidates for an interview.

Be thorough in your questioning when interviewing. All references should be followed up. If you are not completely satisfied with the level of applicants, advertise again until you find the right person. Although this may leave the business short-handed it is probably best in the long run.

Once you have identified a suitable employee you should prepare a contract of employment for him or her to sign. This should outline the duties the employee will be expected to carry out. The contract should cover such matters as:

- hours of work;
- holidays;
- sick pay;
- pension;
- length of notice (from both parties);
- frequency and mode of payment;
- rates of pay;
- disciplinary and grievance procedures.

The document should clearly state the employee's and the employer's name and the date the employment commenced, and must be presented within two months of the date when the employee started work.

It is unlikely that you will be fortunate enough to find an employee who can step into a job and work efficiently straight away. You must be prepared to train your employees. After all, even if you employ a qualified and experienced secretary you will still have to explain where things are kept and how you want things done. Training can be carried out internally, on the job, by you or other experienced employees, or it can be provided by local colleges or by professional training firms.

Most people start a new job with a great deal of enthusiasm. To keep them interested in the job and performing well, they need to be motivated and contented. Staff motivation and contentment can be promoted in a variety of ways. Tips here include:

- If you appreciate your staff let them know it.
- Consider showing your appreciation by giving something tangible such as a bonus, gift or outing.
- Where appropriate set high but achievable targets. Stimulate competition.
- Listen to what your staff say. They know what is going on. They may have good ideas, or they may be dissatisfied about something.
- Make sure you communicate clearly and politely with your staff. Often mistakes made by employees result from employers not explaining matters properly.

The Employment Service listed in your local telephone directory can provide you with useful, free advice on recruiting staff and on employment legislation. If you are employing people who are self-employed, make sure that they are genuinely self-employed or you could end up with a larger than expected tax bill. If you have any doubts contact your local Inland Revenue.

What if it gets a little lonely?

One of the drawbacks of working from home can be a lack of human contact. This can be lonely. It can also mean that there is little business support and can ultimately lead to a dearth of business information and ideas. To lessen these problems consider joining local business gatherings such as the Chamber of Commerce, computer business chat rooms or e-mail which can make you feel more in touch with the business world. The Internet and e-mail are discussed in Chapter 18.

17 *Financial security*

Why is financial security important?

If the profits from your business, together with any other income you have, cannot meet your expenditure, you will be unable to pay all your bills. This can be worrying and stressful. In addition, many home-based operations will provide fluctuating profits, making certain times of the year financially difficult. Financial problems can be heightened or even created by unforeseen events such as illness, accident or a market recession. To alleviate such problems it is important to plan ahead. The financial security needs of both the business and its owner should be reviewed regularly to ensure that their changing require-ments are met. Investigate thoroughly the need for:

- insurance;
- life assurance;
- pensions;
- savings;
- health insurance.

Why is insurance necessary?

Insurance can provide for recompense where accidents, damage, natural disasters or injuries arise. If you are not insured against mishaps or other eventualities, your business may not survive. For example, a delivery service would struggle if it could not replace its only delivery vehicle promptly after an accident. The need for insurance will vary according to the nature of the risks associated with the business you operate. If you have little to lose you may feel that insurance is not necessary.

What types of insurance are there?

Insurance can be obtained for almost any eventuality, so take a good look at your business to assess the risks associated with it. Any significant risk should be covered by insurance. The main type of insurance for a home-based business to consider include:

- personal insurance;
- motor vehicle insurance;
- material damage and consequential loss;
- employer's liability;
- public liability;
- product liability;
- credit insurance;
- loss of money.

Personal insurance

Many businesses, particularly those that are based in the home, would experience severe trading difficulties if the owner or a key employee was unable to work as a result, for instance, of illness or an accident. A personal insurance policy could be taken out to cover such an eventuality.

Motor vehicle insurance

All business vehicles will require, as a legal minimum, third party insurance, but it would be wise to be covered for fire and theft as well. Fully comprehensive insurance, although expensive, can be worthwhile if the motor vehicle is essential to your business. If you are using your own car for business purposes it is important to check with your insurers that your policy covers this situation.

Asset damage and consequential loss

Most firms will feel it necessary to insure themselves against damage to or loss of assets caused by such disasters as burglaries, fire, floods and vandalism. It is important that the proprietor of a home-based business does not assume that his or her business will be covered by the house insurance. Running a business from home may invalidate this, so consult your insurer before you start.

Damage to business assets could result in a reduction of trade or a temporary, even permanent, cessation of trade. This will cause a loss of profits. It is therefore sensible to insure against the loss of the assets and any consequential loss of profits, particularly if you are financially dependent upon those profits.

Employer's liability insurance

This is a legal requirement if you have any non-family, non-domestic employees. It will cover you for claims from employees who have suffered injury or illness as a result of their employment.

Although not legally required, it would be morally fair and reassuring to include any family members you employ.

Public liability insurance

This insurance will cover you for injury claims made by the public in cases where the injury was a result of your actions or your employees' actions at work.

Product liability, professional indemnity

Product liability insurance will provide cover where a product made or serviced by your business has a fault. Where you are providing a service, it may be possible to obtain professional indemnity for claims made as a result of a faulty service.

Credit insurance

Credit insurance offers cover against bad debts. Those businesses that rely heavily on a few major customers are particularly vulnerable. As the risk of bad debts can be high, insurance firms will often provide credit insurance only to established businesses with a good track record of debt collection as part of a commercial insurance package.

Loss of money insurance

If you deal regularly with substantial sums of cash, cheques or postal orders, a loss of money insurance policy is essential. Such a policy can, for example, provide cover for loss of money in transit or in your home.

Your insurance cost will depend upon the level of cover you require and the risks associated with the events against which you are insuring.

Why is life assurance important?

If you have dependants it is important to provide for them in the event of your death. It is best to provide cover to enable your dependants to pay off any debts, such as a business loan, and have sufficient income to live on.

You may already have some life assurance cover; almost certainly your mortgage is covered. Many employers will provide cover where incidents occur during the course of employment. If you are employed check to see if there are any benefits arising from your employment. Once you have established the cover you have, you should top it up so that it is sufficient to cover your estimated needs.

Some life assurance policies can be enhanced to provide for injuries that arise from accidents, thus giving extra security.

Why worry about a pension?

Under the current regulations the NIC you pay will provide you with a state pension when you reach retirement age. However, many people consider this to be insufficient for their requirements and make additional provision.

If you have full- or part-time employment, as well as running your business, you may already be in a company pension scheme to which you contribute. Often, in addition to your payments, the company will contribute on your behalf. Such schemes are usually better value than personal pension plans. If you leave a company pension scheme you may have the option to transfer your contributions to another pension scheme.

When choosing a personal pension scheme it will be necessary to do thorough research to identify the schemes that meet your needs and are good value for money.

If you are an employee, a director for example, you are allowed to pay up to 15 per cent of your net relevant earnings into a company occupational pension scheme or up to 40 per cent into a personal pension scheme (depending on age) or up to £3,600 pa for stakeholder pensions. Net relevant earnings, broadly speaking, are earnings, such as income from a trade, profession, office or employment, which is not already subject to a pension. Most home-based companies are unlikely to provide their own company pension scheme.

Sole traders and partners are allowed to pay up to 40 per cent (depending upon age) of their net relevant earnings into a pension scheme. Pension payments into an Inland Revenue approved scheme are an allowable deduction for taxation purposes.

The percentage of net relevant earnings that can be paid into a personal pension scheme is 17½ per cent for those aged under 36. For other age groups the percentages are:

36–45	20 per cent
46–50	25 per cent
51–55	30 per cent
56–60	35 per cent
61–74	40 per cent
75 and over	Nil

There is a permitted maximum of 95,400 for the tax year 2001/02.

What is a stakeholder pension?

Stakeholder pensions are low-cost (up to 1 per cent per annum of the funds invested can be charged), flexible pensions allowing members to stop and start their contributions (after six months' notice).

Must my business start a pension scheme?

Businesses with five or more employees will be obliged to provide access to a pension scheme for its employees (schemes must be operational by 8 October 2001). Employees include directors, partners, sole traders and part-time staff. The scheme can be a:

- final salary occupational scheme;
- group personal pension;
- stakeholder pension.

Is it necessary to save?

Savings provide a measure of security against hard times. The larger your savings the greater the degree of security. Your personal savings can be used to carry you through a bad patch in your business or through any personal financial upheavals, such as a family wedding or funeral.

If your business generates surplus funds these can also be invested, either in the business to purchase equipment or extra stock, in an interest-bearing account or shares to generate extra income. When you are investing make sure that you choose a suitable investment vehicle. Those that tie up your money for a longer period will yield higher returns but are less flexible. It may be appropriate to split up your savings into a number of investments to ensure that you obtain a good average return while keeping some of your money easily accessible.

Is health insurance essential?

Probably not. Its main advantage is that any non-urgent medical treatment can be more easily timed to suit you and your business.

It is important, however, to look after your health. It can be difficult to take a proper holiday when you are running your own business. Unless you can find a trustworthy person to hold the fort while you are away it will be necessary to close down. Either option, through extra salaries or lost profits, will hit your pocket, but a holiday can lead to improved health and a fresh outlook when you return to work, so that in the long run your business is likely to benefit.

Relaxation can also play an important role in keeping you mentally and physically fit. This can be more difficult for the home-based worker since you are never far from your work. Hobbies or interests away from the home can help. Courses in relaxation can often be found by checking local newspapers or by contacting local colleges.

Will it be possible to obtain a mortgage?

Rules and regulations for obtaining a mortgage are continually changing. If you search around you will find different requirements, limitations and repayment rates. Many lenders will wish to see some accounts to confirm your level of profits.

Running your own business?

How long can you afford to wait for treatment if you're ill?

- 2 weeks?
- 1 month?
- 3 months?
- 6 months?
- 9 months?
- 1 year?

Because you're running your own business, if you become ill and the wait for treatment is long, your life may be affected in many ways. Having to take extended time off work could have a very serious impact on your business.

Don't take a chance, take out quality medical cover with PPP healthcare.

We have a wide range of plans to suit most people's healthcare needs, and budgets. And each offers a superb selection of benefits such as:

- **Prompt access** to private in-patient hospital treatment of all new eligible medical conditions arising after you join.

- **No overall annual limit** to the total amount you can claim.

- **£50 cash tax-free** for every night you spend in hospital as an NHS patient, for treatment that your policy would have covered.

- Hospital bills **settled direct** - so you're not out of pocket.

- **Health at Hand, 24 hour health information service** - staffed by qualified medical experts 365 days a year.

Another good reason to join... when you take out a plan with PPP you'll receive your **first month's cover free**.

For a no obligation personal quotation, or immediate cover, call today on:

0800 33 55 55
Ask for extension 9360

Lines open 8am - 8pm weekdays, 9am - 1pm Saturdays

Calls may be recorded in case of subsequent query.

PPP is a member of the General Insurance Standards Council.

PPP healthcare

Member of the Global AXA Group

18   *The electronic office*

Technology is continually changing and improving. Innovations such as the Internet, e-mail and electronic banking are of particular interest to the home-based business as they provide flexibility, information and improved communication.

What is the Internet?

A global computer network. That is, in layman's terms, a lot of computers across the world joined together. This gives Internet subscribers access to worldwide information and to one another. The information available includes:

- price lists;
- product details;
- services, such as product support;
- adverts;
- tax regulations;
- other government information sites.

Such information can be useful for market research.

The Internet can also be used to:

- download software;
- choose, order and pay for goods and services;
- download forms (eg the change of company address form from the Companies House Web site);
- submit tax returns;
- converse in chat rooms.

Should a home-based business subscribe to the Internet?

The Internet offers a lot to the home-based business:

- 24-hour access to information;
- a wide range of information;
- the ability to provide information to actual and potential customers 24 hours a day;
- a chance to keep in touch with the business world;
- the potential for quick document and transaction completion;
- a useful marketing tool;
- the chance to sell to customers around the clock.

Such benefits should be weighed up against:

- the cost of the equipment, software and subscriptions (where appropriate the incremental cost can be relatively low);
- the time required to identify relevant information;
- the relevance of the benefits to your business, its customers and its suppliers;
- set-up time, particularly if you are new to the Web.

How can I gain access to the Internet?

Before committing yourself to joining the Internet it would be wise to investigate carefully. Computer retailers will provide help, information and a chance to 'surf the Internet' (browse through the available information). The necessary equipment – a telephone line, a suitable computer such as a PC, communications modem and software – can be bought or rented. Some libraries offer facilities to the public.

How can I sell to my customers using the Internet?

To be able to sell on the Internet you need to produce and host a Web site. A Web site is a page or more of text and pictures that can be viewed by customers who have Web access. To successfully sell to your customers, you need to attract them to your Web site and then convince them to buy from you. A Web site can be used to sell directly to your customers or to advertise the goods and services your business offers and other methods of buying from you.

How do I produce a Web site?

You can produce a Web site yourself using a package such as Microsoft Front Page or similar. Alternatively, you could employ a Web designer to do it for you. If you wish your site to be an online shop where customers can view, order and pay for your goods online, then it will require additional programming or the purchase of some specialist software, such as Actinic, and an account with a payment service provider, such as Securetrading or Worldpay, which provides online real-time authorisation of credit cards.

How do I get my site on the Web?

To do this, you need to have a Web hosting account. This means hiring space on an Internet service provider's server, on to which you can upload your Web site. Once you have done this, your Web site will be available to the world. There are many Web-hosting companies that offer this service. Shop around to compare prices and services. One essential factor is a reliable support service.

What should my Web site look like?

A Web site needs to be easy to follow, attractive, informative and reassuring. It also needs to be quick to download or customers will lose interest. The precise details you give will depend on the purpose of your site, for example, whether you are merely advertising your business or aiming to sell online. It is important to ensure that your customer is aware who you are (your business name), where you are (contact details; telephone number, address, e-mail) and what your VAT registration number is if applicable. Other information to consider includes:

- business history;
- description of products and services;
- reassurance of payment security (your site should offer encryption of credit card details and offer other methods of payment to the nervous);
- terms and conditions (at the point of sale, customers can be asked to tick a box indicating that they accept the terms and conditions before an order is processed);
- details of any guarantees you are offering;
- replies to frequently asked questions (FAQs).

How do I get my customers to see my Web site?

If you want customers to visit your Web site, then they need to know about it! A good starting point is to:

- Put your Web address on all your documentation and include it in any advertising;

- Register with a good search engine. A search engine will be used by people to search for information, products or services they are interested in, but for which they do not have a Web address. There are businesses that will register you with the search engines and keep the listing up to date.
- Identify complementary sites that may be interested in having mutual hyperlinks with your site. A hyperlink, when clicked on, will take you directly to another site (many Web sites will offer a disclaimer at these links so that people are aware who is responsible for each site).
- Choose a suitable domain name.
- Advertise and promote the Web site.
- Give the customers an incentive to visit your site. For example, an accountant might include a section giving free tax tips.

What is a domain name?

A domain name is also known as a Web address or URL and is a bit like a telephone number or postal address. When customers enter your domain name into their browser, they will be taken to the Web site that the domain name points to.

Which domain name should I use?

There are two elements to consider. The particular name you desire (eg businessbooks4sale) and the domain you would like to register with (eg .com, .net or .co.uk). It is worthwhile giving both elements of the name plenty of consideration. The name might suggest the nature of your business or be close to your business name. The best names are easy to remember and quick to type. Which domain you choose will depend on a number of factors:

- .coms are currently the most popular and hint at the business being international;

- .co.uk is a cheap popular option for businesses in this country;
- .ltd.uk is only available to the limited company of the same name;
- others to choose from include .it, .gb.com and .gb.net;
- some registries have restrictions, such as requiring a legal presence in the registry's country.

Many businesses will register more than one name, all of which point to the same business Web site.

Where can I buy a domain name?

There are many domain name registration businesses selling domain names on the Web (eg Simply Names Limited at www.simplynames. co.uk, which has an informative Web site for those new to this area). Plenty also advertise in computer magazines. When deciding who to buy from, compare prices and the services that are included. As far as possible, establish the business's credentials because if it folds you could end up paying more than you had bargained for. Make sure that you or your company are the registrant and not the company doing the registration.

How can I avoid fraud on the Internet?

As with any transaction, it is impossible to completely eradicate fraud. However, there are steps you can take to reduce your risk:

- As far as possible, try to establish who you are dealing with. Look at their Web site for contact details – try to find more than just an e-mail address. If you are dealing with a limited company, details can be checked on the Companies House Web site: www.companieshouse.co.uk. Phone or write to them using the details given.
- Discuss the security measures offered by your payment services provider to combat fraud.

- Digital security certificates offer an encrypted digital key, which can authenticate who you are dealing with.
- Observe unusual ordering patterns.

What is e-mail?

E-mail is short for electronic mail. Where computers are connected and the relevant software is installed it is possible to send documents electronically from computer to computer. This could be done within the same firm or between different businesses. The documents (eg letters, orders, invoices) can then be stored electronically or printed out. To save time a document can be created once and mailed to numerous e-mail addresses.

E-mail speeds up business communication, can be used 24 hours a day and can save time and storage space. The relevance of e-mail to a business will largely depend on the nature of the business, its customers and suppliers. E-mail can ease differences in language and time when dealing with overseas customers.

What is electronic banking?

As with the Internet and e-mail, the banks and building societies are using technology to speed up communication, reduce paperwork and introduce flexible access to services. For example, financial services such as loans can be dealt with over the Internet and home finance packages are now available. These are designed to offer facilities such as direct access to a customer's account.

Many banks now offer PC access to account information and will allow you to make transactions such as sending payments or transferring funds, from the comfort of your own home or office. Details of other financial services, such as loans and mortgages, are also now being provided on the Internet together with the ability to apply online.

19 *The future*

When is it time to change?

This is something only you and your family can decide. Changes will have to be considered when the business needs to contract, expand, move or diversify. Alternatively, your personal life may dictate some business changes, for example ill health, retirement, an expanding family or boredom. The changes that result are likely to fall into the following categories:

- expansion of the business;
- relocation of the business;
- a change in the business's aims and objectives;
- sale of the business.

When should I sell the business?

You are likely to consider selling up under the following conditions:

- when suffering ill health;
- when nearing retirement;
- if the business is performing badly and providing insufficient income;

- if you are no longer, personally, satisfied with the work you are doing and feel you need a new challenge.

Do not rush your decision, but consider all the options open to you:

- sell part of the business so that the work is now part-time;
- take on a partner or employ a manager;
- merge with another business;
- change your business operation;
- diversify.

How much should I sell the business for?

As with a house, the valuation of a business is a problematic and subjective area. At the end of the day a business is worth what someone else is prepared to pay for it. The amount someone is prepared to pay for a business will be based upon:

- how much they can afford to pay;
- how closely the firm meets their requirements;
- the assets that are included in the sale;
- the amount of any liabilities that are to be transferred to the new owner;
- the level of profit the business is making;
- the level of profit the business is expected to continue making;
- the quality of the customers (for example, prompt paying and repeat orders);
- the number of customers expected to buy elsewhere due to the change in ownership;
- the level of competition from other interested buyers which pushes up the price of the firm.

A number of accounting techniques can be used to help estimate business valuations. These techniques will calculate valuations around which negotiations can be carried out and involve using accounting theories and making assumptions. The results should be treated with caution. The following valuation methods will be considered:

- net assets valuation;
- accounting rate of return.

These two methods will give an indication of the maximum and minimum price for which you can expect to sell your business. The rest will be down to negotiation.

Net assets valuation

This values the business at an amount equivalent to its net assets. The net assets figure is calculated by deducting total liabilities from total assets. When estimating total assets the following should be taken into account:

- The need for professional evaluation of the assets. The larger the value of the asset the more likely it is that professional advice will be necessary. Most home-based businesses are unlikely to have high-value assets because these are usually premises, large machines or large motor vehicles.
- The value of debtors should take account of any amounts that are unlikely to be received and any credit notes that need to be issued.
- Stock values should be based on the condition of the stock and how saleable it is. A stock count, as carried out at the end of the year, would be an appropriate way of establishing stock quantities.
- When estimating liabilities make sure that all liabilities that will accrue to the new owner are included. A buyer may include future expected liabilities, such as redundancy costs, or possible pending litigation.

This method of valuation does not take into account any goodwill built up by the business. Goodwill can be created by:

- good customer relations;
- a good reputation;
- good employee relations.

A valuation based on net asset values will, therefore, produce a low value and should represent the minimum acceptable price for the business.

The accounting rate of return valuation

The formula used is:

$$\text{Valuation} = \frac{\text{Estimated future profits per annum}}{\text{Required return on capital employed}}$$

When estimating future profits, past performance, future prospects, current trends and any known changes should be considered. It can be quite difficult to place a figure on the required rate of return on capital employed. As there are risks associated with business the rate is almost certain to be in excess of building society and bank investors' interest rates.

The following example illustrates the calculation. The future profits of a mail order business are expected to average £7,500 per annum. The desired rate of return on capital employed is 25 per cent, therefore:

$$\text{Valuation} = \frac{7,500}{0.25} = £30,000$$

This method of valuation will give a guide as to the upper limit of the amount for which you can expect to sell.

The above techniques provide a useful guide when selling a home-based business. They are, therefore, also useful when purchasing a business.

How can I sell the business?

To sell your business, you need to bring it to the attention of people who may be interested in buying it. There are a number of ways of doing this:

- Advertise the business, perhaps in the local press or a specialist journal.
- Use a business transfer agent.
- Inform your professional advisers (accountant, solicitor). They may have contacts with people who are interested in buying a business.
- Consider letting your competitors and other business contacts know of your decision to sell as they may be interested in purchasing your business or have contacts who are.

Selling a business takes time. If you are not in a rush to sell you are more likely to achieve your asking price.

What are the tax consequences of selling a home-based business?

The sale of a business could generate a capital gains tax liability. If the gain, when you sell, is over £7,500 (this amount is subject to review in the Budget) a liability will arise.

If the amount of tax looks like being significant the advice of a qualified accountant should be sought. When the sale is made on the grounds of retirement, ill health, or the proceeds are to be reinvested in another business, there may be relief from, or allowable delay in payment of, capital gains tax.

When will the business need to expand?

Expansion can be gradual or sudden. It might be temporary or permanent. The expansion, whatever its nature, will be created by increased orders and sales. It is, therefore, up to you to decide when and by how much you wish to expand and then to set about achieving it.

What are the consequences of expansion?

Expansion is usually considered to be good for a business: extra sales should provide extra profit. Although this is true, there can be some drawbacks.

The main drawback for a home-based business will probably be lack of space. More sales imply more storage and manufacturing space. At the very least the paperwork generated will require filing space.

It is very important that any business expansion is planned and controlled. Prepare a cash flow forecast. The increase in sales will almost certainly require additional finance. More labour and materials will be needed and have to be paid for before the sales income is received. It may be necessary to raise further finance. This should be organised before the expansion is under way, otherwise it could be too late. An under-financed expansion could cause severe cash flow problems, even bankruptcy or liquidation.

As the business grows it will become increasingly difficult for you to keep it under tight control. It may become necessary to devolve running parts of the business to staff who have, in the past, proved trustworthy. Such staff will need to be well trained if your business standards are to be maintained.

The nature of a growing business may also change and it may be necessary to review:

- selling prices;
- marketing strategy;
- sales methods;
- advertising;
- bookkeeping;
- registration for VAT.

Expansion is not necessarily an easy route to greater profits. The consequences of business growth should be scrutinised before embarking on the road to expansion.

Why relocate a business?

A home-based business may need to relocate because it has expanded and now requires business premises or the owner may be moving home for family reasons.

When relocating it is important to ensure that everyone who needs to contact the business is aware of the change of address. If possible keep the same telephone number.

In addition to ensuring that your customers and suppliers are aware of the changes you must also notify the Inland Revenue, Customs and Excise, your accountant and any other professional advisers. Limited companies must inform the Registrar of Companies of any change in their registered office on an official form.

If the move is over some distance or involves a change of area, it may be necessary to consider additional market research and advertising. Do not assume that a move will have little effect on your sales. A change of address for a delivery service may have little impact but moving a hairdressing business 10 miles would probably require you to start from scratch again.

Of course, there are benefits associated with moving. For example, a move to a more populated area may offer the opportunity for increased sales. If you move to improve your business potential it is important to research all the implications of the move thoroughly. It is as important to understand how your current customers will react to your move as it is to anticipate the reaction of potential customers in the new area.

Any move can cause practical problems for the home-based business. Anyone who has moved house can comprehend the turmoil, disruption and frustration that a business move can cause. The problems will be compounded if, at the same time, you are moving home.

Unless the move is carefully organised there could be serious repercussions for the business. Sales invoices could be lost, stock damaged, information about debtors mislaid and deliveries delayed. Such problems will worsen the business's cash flow and reduce profits.

To minimise the difficulties:

- plan the move for a quiet time of year;
- avoid sales shortly before and after the move;
- keep all business records accessible and separate from personal belongings;
- consider employing help in the business and for the removal;
- be organised well in advance.

Business premises

If your home-based business has proved very successful you might find it necessary to move into business premises, which may well be a new experience for you. Choosing the wrong premises can be a very costly mistake. Often a long-term commitment is required and this can tie your business to the premises for a number of years.

It will be prudent to carry out some market research on the premises, particularly if it is a retail outlet or needs to be readily accessible to customers. The lack of nearby, cheap parking can be detrimental to a shop's chances of success. It is also important to select premises that will meet your business needs both now and for the foreseeable future or at least can be adapted to meet those needs.

A major expansion such as moving premises should be carefully planned. All the financial implications must be considered. It will be necessary to decide whether to buy, rent or lease the premises. There will be additional overheads such as rates and insurance to be paid. This will require additional finance. Prices will need to be reviewed, taking into account all the relevant factors (for example competitors). It may be necessary to increase prices unless sales are expected to increase sufficiently to cover the extra costs.

Finally, before signing any contract, particularly if it is for a lease, take legal advice. Make sure you understand the implications of the commitments you are making. You should also consider the problems and costs you may encounter if, at some stage in the future, you no longer require the premises.

When should aims and objectives be changed?

What you want to achieve with your business should be continually under review. You may have financial targets to meet or service standards to attain. Once these have been met, set more.

Without aims and objectives a business can meander along achieving very little. A major change to the aims and objectives of a business could enable it to meet changed personal aims and objectives.

Sources of further information

Chapters 1 to 3

Chatterton, Peter (1999) *Your Home Office: A practical guide to using technology successfully*, 3rd edn, Kogan Page, London

Clarke, Greg (1999) *Buying Your First Franchise*, 3rd edn, Kogan Page, London

Clayton, Patricia (2001) *Forming a Limited Company*, 7th edn, Kogan Page, London

Grappo, Gary Joseph (1998) *Start Your Own Business in 30 Days*, Kogan Page, London

Morris, Michael J (2001) *Starting a Successful Business*, 4th edn, Kogan Page, London

Chapter 4

Ali, Moi (1998) *Practical Marketing and PR for the Small Business*, Kogan Page, London

Barrow, Colin (2001) *Financial Management for the Small Business*, 5th edn, Kogan Page

Barrow, Colin, Barrow, Paul and Brown, Robert (2001) *The Business Plan Workbook*, 4th edn, Kogan Page, London

Finch, Brian (1998) *Business Plans: 45 ways to make yours more successful*, 2nd edn, Kogan Page, London

Finch, Brian (2001) *How to Write a Business Plan*, Kogan Page, London

Forsyth, Patrick (2000) *Marketing on a Tight Budget: An action guide to low-cost business growth*, Kogan Page, London

Westwood, John (2000) *How to Write a Marketing Plan*, 2nd edn, Kogan Page, London

Chapters 5 and 6

Patten, Dave (2001) *Successful Marketing for the Small Business*, 5th edn, Kogan Page

Chapter 8

Shavick, Andrea (1998) *The Cheque's In the Post: Credit control for the small business*, Kogan Page, London

Chapters 9 and 10

The Kogan Page 'Simple and Practical' Series provides easy-to-follow, useful advice for people in small businesses, and feature exercises, self-test questions and fully worked examples. Also, they come with a free Sage disk, a 30-day trial CD ROM containing a full version of the Sage Instant Accounts and Instant Payroll Packages.

Chesworth, Niki (1998) *Self-Assessment for the Small Business and The Self-Employed*, Kogan Page, London

Fisher, John G (2001) *E-Business for the Small Business*, Kogan Page, London

Green, Jim (2001) *Starting an Internet Business at Home: How to make easy money on the Web*, Kogan Page, London

Haig, Matt (2001) *E-Business Essentials*, Kogan Page, London

Mott, Graham (1999) *Accounting for Non-Accountants*, 5th edn, Kogan Page, London

Price, A St John (1999) *Understand Your Accounts*, 4th edn, Kogan Page, London

Sperry, Paul S and Mitchell, Beatrice H (1999) *The Complete Guide to Selling Your Business*, Kogan Page, London

Chapter 13

Clayton, Patricia (2001) *Forming a Limited Company*, 7th edn, Kogan
   Page, London
Clayton, Patricia (2001) *Law for the Small Business*, 10th edn, Kogan
   Page, London

Periodicals

Home Business and Your Business

Home Run

The New Entrepreneur (TNE)

Useful addresses

Business in the Community
137 Shepherdess Walk
London N1 7RQ
Tel: 0870 600 2482
Web site: www.bitc.org.uk

Federation of Small Businesses
Whittle Way
Blackpool Business Park
Blackpool
Lancashire FY4 2FE
Tel: 01253 336000
Fax: 01253 348046
Web site: www.fsb.org.uk

The Forum of Private Business Ltd
Ruskin Chambers
Drury Lane
Knutsford
Cheshire WA16 6HA
Tel: 01565 634468
E-mail: fpbltd@fpb.co.uk
Web site: www.fpb.co.uk

Index

NB: numbers in italics indicate figures and tables

Index of advertisers